Pressure Cookers For Dummies®

P9-DTO-498

Cheat Sheet

Tips for Successful Pressure Cooking

Follow these tips for the best pressure cooking results:

- **Brown meats, poultry, and even some vegetables — like chopped onions, peppers, or carrots — first and then deglaze the pot for more intense flavor.** Add a small amount of oil, such as olive or canola oil, to the pressure cooker and heat, uncovered, over medium-high heat. Add the food in small batches and brown the food on all sides. Remove and deglaze the pan with a small amount of wine, broth, or even water. Add the remaining ingredients and cook under pressure. (See Chapter 3.)

- **Don't overdo the liquid.** Because food cooks in a closed, sealed pot when cooking under pressure, you'll have less evaporation and should therefore use less cooking liquid than when cooking in a conventional pot. Regardless of what you're cooking, however, always use enough liquid. A good rule of thumb is at least 1 cup of liquid, however, check the owner's manual or recipe booklet to see exactly what the pressure cooker manufacturer recommends. It's also important to remember that the pot should never be filled more than halfway with liquid. (See Chapter 2.)

- **Don't fill the pressure cooker with too much food.** Never fill the pressure cooker more than two-thirds full with food. Never pack the food tightly into the pressure cooker. (See Chapter 2.)

- **Even pieces mean evenly cooked food.** Food should be cut into uniform-sized pieces so that they cook in the same amount of time. (See Chapter 3.)

- **Use stop-and-go batch cooking for perfect results.** When making a recipe that contains ingredients that cook at different times, begin by partially cooking slow-to-cook foods such as meat first. Then use a quick-release method to stop the pressure cooker. Next, add the faster-cooking ingredients — such as green beans or peas — to the meat. Bring the pot back up to pressure again and finish everything up together at the same time. (See Chapter 3.)

- **Start off high and finish up low.** Bring the pressure cooker up to pressure over high heat. Cook under pressure at a simmer. (See Chapter 2.)

- **Play burner hopscotch to avoid burning.** Once you reach pressure over high heat, you lower the burner to a simmer. Gas burners react quickly, but most electric burners don't. If you have an electric stove, use two burners: one on high heat to reach pressure and a second set on a low setting to maintain it. Switch the pressure cooker over to the burner with the low setting when you reach pressure. (See Chapter 2.)

- **Set a timer.** Once the pressure cooker reaches and maintains pressure, have a kitchen timer handy and set it for the cooking time specified in the recipe or in the recommended cooking time chart. (See Chapter 2.)

- **High altitude means longer cooking times.** You may have to increase the cooking times if you live at an elevation of 3,000 feet above sea level or higher. (See Chapter 13.)

- **Release that pressure.** When the food is done cooking under pressure, use an appropriate pressure release method, according to the recipe you're making. (See Chapter 2.)

For Dummies: Bestselling Book Series for Beginners

Pressure Cookers For Dummies®

Cheat Sheet

Suggested Pressure Cooker Cooking Times

The following cooking times begin when the pressure cooker reaches high pressure. Always start with the shortest cooking time; you can always continue cooking under pressure for an additional couple minutes until the desired texture is reached.

Food	Cooking Time (in Minutes)	Food	Cooking Time (in Minutes)
Apples, chunks	2	Corn on the cob	3 to 4
Artichokes, whole	8 to 10	Meat (beef, pork, or lamb), roast	40 to 60
Asparagus, whole	1 to 2	Meat (beef, pork, or lamb), 1-inch cubes	15 to 20
Barley, pearl	15 to 20	Peas, shelled	1 to 1½
Beans, fresh green or wax, whole or pieces	2 to 3	Potatoes, pieces or sliced	5 to 7
Beans, lima, shelled	2 to 3	Potatoes, whole, medium	10 to 12
Beets, ¼-inch slices	3 to 4	Potatoes, whole, small or new	5 to 7
Beets, whole, peeled	12 to 14	Rice, brown	15 to 20
Broccoli, florets or spears	2 to 3	Rice, white	5 to 7
Brussels sprouts, whole	3 to 4	Spinach, fresh	2 to 3
Cabbage, red or green, quartered	3 to 4	Squash, fall, 1-inch chunks	4 to 6
Carrots, ¼-inch slices	1 to 2	Squash, summer, sliced	1 to 2
Cauliflower, florets	2 to 3	Stock	30
Chicken, pieces	10 to 12	Sweet potatoes, 1½-inch chunks	4 to 5
Chicken, whole	15 to 20	Turnips, sliced	2 to 3

Temperature-Pressure Ratios

Pressure Setting	Cooking Temperature	Pressure Level
High pressure	250 degrees	13-15 psi (pounds per square inch)
Medium pressure	235 degrees	10 psi
Low pressure	220 degrees	3 psi

For Dummies: Bestselling Book Series for Beginners

Pressure Cookers

FOR

DUMMIES®

Pressure Cookers

FOR

DUMMIES®

by Tom Lacalamita

WILEY

Wiley Publishing, Inc.

Pressure Cookers For Dummies®

Published by
Wiley Publishing, Inc.
909 Third Avenue
New York, NY 10022
www.wiley.com

Copyright © 2002 by Wiley Publishing, Inc., Indianapolis, Indiana

Published simultaneously in Canada

No part of this publication may be reproduced, stored in a retrieval system, or transmitted in any form or by any means, electronic, mechanical, photocopying, recording, scanning, or otherwise, except as permitted under Sections 107 or 108 of the 1976 United States Copyright Act, without either the prior written permission of the Publisher, or authorization through payment of the appropriate per-copy fee to the Copyright Clearance Center, 222 Rosewood Drive, Danvers, MA 01923, 978-750-8400, fax 978-750-4470. Requests to the Publisher for permission should be addressed to the Legal Department, Wiley Publishing, Inc., 10475 Crosspoint Blvd., Indianapolis, IN 46256, 317-572-3447, fax 317-572-4447, or e-mail permcoordinator@wiley.com

Trademarks: Wiley, the Wiley Publishing logo, For Dummies, the Dummies Man logo, A Reference for the Rest of Us!, The Dummies Way, Dummies Daily, The Fun and Easy way, Dummies.com and related trade dress are trademarks or registered trademarks of Wiley Publishing, Inc., in the United States and other countries, and may not be used without written permission. All other trademarks are the property of their respective owners. Wiley Publishing, Inc., is not associated with any product or vendor mentioned in this book.

For general information on our other products and services or to obtain technical support, please contact our Customer Care Department within the U.S. at 800-762-2974, outside the U.S. at 317-572-3993, or fax 317-572-4002.

Wiley also publishes its books in a variety of electronic formats. Some content that appears in print may not be available in electronic books.

Library of Congress Cataloging-in-Publication Data:

Library of Congress Control Number: 2001092903

ISBN: 0-7645-5413-1

Manufactured in the United States of America

10 9 8 7 6 5 4 3

1B/ST/QR/QT/IN

About the Author

Tom Lacalamita (Long Island, NY) is a bestselling author of five appliance-related cookbooks. Nominated for a James Beard cookbook award, Lacalamita is considered to be a national authority on housewares and has appeared on hundreds of television and radio shows across the country. With a passion for food, cooking, and all sorts of kitchen gadgets, Tom is also a spokesperson for various food and housewares manufacturers.

Publisher's Acknowledgments

We're proud of this book; please send us your comments through our online registration form located at www.dummies.com/register.

Some of the people who helped bring this book to market include the following:

Acquisitions, Editorial, and Media Development

Project Editor: Suzanne Snyder

Senior Acquisitions Editor: Linda Ingroia

Senior Copy Editor: Tina Sims

Assistant Acquisitions Coordinator: Erin Connell

Technical Editor: Marjorie Cubisino

Recipe Tester: Emily Nolan

Nutritional Analyst: Patty Santelli

Editorial Manager: Pam Mourouzis

Editorial Assistant: Carol Strickland

Cover Photos: Art Director, Edwin Kuo; Photographer, David Bishop; Food Stylist, Brett Kurzweil; Prop Stylist, Randi Barritt

Production

Project Coordinator: Regina Snyder

Layout and Graphics: Amy Adrian, Clint Lahnen, Jacque Schneider, Jeremey Unger, Erin Zeltner

Special Art: Liz Kurtzman

Proofreaders: TECHBOOKS Production Services

Indexer: TECHBOOKS Production Services

Publishing and Editorial for Consumer Dummies

Diane Graves Steele, Vice President and Publisher, Consumer Dummies
Joyce Pepple, Acquisitions Director, Consumer Dummies
Kristin A. Cocks, Product Development Director, Consumer Dummies
Michael Spring, Vice President and Publisher, Travel
Brice Gosnell, Publishing Director, Travel
Suzanne Jannetta, Editorial Director, Travel

Publishing for Technology Dummies

Richard Swadley, Vice President and Executive Group Publisher
Andy Cummings, Vice President and Publisher

Composition Services

Gerry Fahey, Vice President of Production Services
Debbie Stailey, Director of Composition Services

Contents at a Glance

Cartoons at a Glance

By Rich Tennant

page 7

page 63

page 149

page 33

page 187

Cartoon Information:
Fax: 978-546-7747
E-Mail: richtennant@the5thwave.com
World Wide Web: www.the5thwave.com

Recipes at a Glance

Master Recipes

Salads

Sauces and Spreads

Soups, Chowders, and Chili

Stews

Table of Contents

Introduction

The pressure cooker is one kitchen appliance that's long been misunderstood and underappreciated. Maligned for decades and the brunt of endless jokes and unwarranted stories, this kitchen wonder survived for years, once truly appreciated only by people in the know. Today's sleek, fast-cooking pressure cookers, however, have safety valves and other features that make them totally safe and easy to use — a far cry from the ones used decades ago.

Wouldn't you like to have savory, delicious, homemade beef stew cooked in under 45 minutes, compared to 90 minutes of simmering and stirring the old-fashioned way? What about nutritious dried beans or legumes that normally need to simmer up to 2 hours but can be yours in less than 20 minutes? Whet your appetite? By cooking with a pressure cooker, you can have these fast and tasty foods and more.

Why You Need This Book

Chances are, you've probably never used a pressure cooker, or if you have, you still may still have some questions or a few misconceptions about this gadget. So join me as I demystify pressure cookers and explain how they really work and what to expect as far as delicious home-cooked foods are concerned. In fact, I share with you some of the all-time-best pressure cooker recipes I know.

How to Use This Book

Although the beginning is usually a good place to start, books about cooking are different. You should be able to pick up and start reading wherever you want, so that's exactly the goal I had in mind when I wrote this book. Looking for a great pot roast recipe? Turn to Chapter 7, which contains information about making roasts and other large cuts of meat in your pressure cooker. Wondering how to make quick and easy jams and chutney for holiday gift giving? Then be sure to check out my recipes in Chapter 10.

Because I hope that you will soon rely upon your pressure cooker for quick and easily prepared foods, I suggest you become well acquainted with your pressure cooker and your pressure cooker manufacturer's documentation to better understand how it works. Naturally, I am proud of all the information I've compiled in this book and hope that you will take the time to read most of it. If you don't initially, that's okay, too, because I know that you'll like the recipes so much that, before you even realize it, you'll have ultimately read almost everything, from cover to cover! Or, if you'd like, you can start anywhere and read as little or as much as you want at a time. After all, it's your book.

Foolish Assumptions

Just because you're reading this introduction to a book about pressure cookers, I can't necessarily assume that you already own a pressure cooker. Some people like to use a book like this one as a guide to find out more about the product before purchasing it. If that's the case, I recommend that you take a look at Chapters 1 and 2, where you're certain to find everything you need to know about pressure cookers. You can also check Appendix A for a list of pressure cooker manufacturers.

How This Book Is Organized

This book is divided into five parts of information. The opening chapters go into detailed product information, as well as use and care information. Because I know that you'll eventually want to be able to adapt some of your favorite recipes for the pressure cooker, I shared with you in Chapter 4 the ins and outs on how to convert them. You also can find other recipes organized in typical cookbook-menu sequence: soups, followed by meat and poultry, vegetables and side dishes, and then desserts. I'm certain that you'll enjoy these recipes as much as I do.

Part 1: Stress-Free Cooking under Pressure

With so many misconceptions surrounding the pressure cooker, I'm going to start off by dispelling them, one at a time! You find out everything you need to know about how pressure cookers work and why tens of millions of people around the world use them every day.

Part II: Making the Best and Safest Use of Your Pressure Cooker

In this part, I fill you in on what to expect as far as features and benefits when cooking under pressure, and why today's new models are safer and easier to use than ever before. I share with you some of the tricks I've learned along the way for getting the best results with the least amount of effort, as well as how to adapt your favorite, conventional recipes for the pressure cooker.

Part III: Getting Dinner on the Table: Basic and Delicious Recipes for the Pressure Cooker

Quick, delicious, homemade food is what pressure cooking is all about, and those are the results (not to mention the compliments) you're bound to get when you make any of the recipes in this section. Part III contains nearly 80 recipes, covering the gamut from flavorful soups to fork-tender pot roasts and stews as well as side dishes, too.

Part IV: Complements to the Meal: Side Dishes, Condiments, and Sweet Endings

Every great meal deserves a delicious side dish and a fabulous dessert. Make family favorites such as old-fashioned mashed potatoes, or how about an exquisite cauliflower and broccoli custard? To top off the meal, choose from a variety of desserts, including creamy cheesecakes, bread pudding, and a fruit crisp, all made in the pressure cooker in no time at all!

Part V: The Part of Tens

Years ago, it was common practice for people to pick up the phone and call Mom with their cooking questions. You can still call Mom today, but you'll probably get her answering machine while she's out playing tennis, taking a class, or hitting the outlet stores. Instead, check out my Part of Tens, where I give you invaluable tips, troubleshooting hints, and Web sites about pressure cookers.

Appendixes

Someday, sometime, something may go wrong, and you'll need to contact the manufacturer with a question or for assistance. Instead of scrambling through old drawers looking for the owner's manual, refer to Appendix A for a complete listing of manufacturers' customer service phone numbers and Web sites, if available. See Appendix B for handy metric and other conversion information, and Appendix C for substitutions abbreviations, and equivalents.

Icons Used in This Book

Icons are symbols or pictures that represent or convey an idea. I use three of them throughout this book where I think an idea or concept should be stressed for your benefit.

Simply stated, this icon points out tips or shortcuts I've picked up over the years that I share with you to make your cooking more fun and less of a hassle.

When you see this icon, I'm warning you about a potential problem or pitfall. Rest assured, I wouldn't warn you without also telling you how to avoid or overcome the problem.

This icon means, "Okay, you've heard this stuff before, but the information's just too important not to give it to you again."

A Few Guidelines before You Begin

We walk before we run, and so goes with everything in life. Because you've taken the time to pick up this book, you're obviously interested in knowing how to use a pressure cooker properly. With this in mind, I give you some pointers to make your life easier before you even start.

✔ Always read a recipe from beginning to end at least once before preparing a dish to make sure that you know how long it's going to take to prepare and cook, what steps and procedures are involved, and what cooking utensils you need.

✔ Have all the ingredients on hand before you start cooking. In fact, just so you don't miss anything, you may want to place all the ingredients on the counter.

✔ All dry ingredient measurements should be level. Spoon the ingredient into the appropriate-sized measuring cup and level off with the blunt edge of a knife. You don't need to pat down the ingredient, because more is not necessarily better than less.

✔ Never overfill the pressure cooker. Your pressure cooker should be no more than half full with solid foods or two-thirds full with liquid when making soups, stocks, or sauces.

✔ Use enough liquid. Use at least 1 cup of liquid when you're cooking in a pressure cooker, although you should check your pressure cooker owner's manual since some call for 2 cups of liquid. Use at least 3 cups of liquid when you're steaming foods in the steaming basket or rack.

✔ Before washing beans and dried legumes, always pick through to remove any foreign objects like pebbles or twigs. Rinse them under cold water and then soak over night in cool water, or for one hour in boiling water, before cooking under pressure. Never salt beans until they are done cooking or the skins will be tough.

✔ You can add a tablespoon of oil to the water to reduce the foaming that beans often cause.

✔ "Preheat" the pressure cooker first. Cooking in a pressure cooker is sort of like making a cake in an oven. First you preheat the oven. Then you place the cake pan in the oven and set the kitchen timer for the suggested baking time. When cooking in a pressure cooker, you put the food in the pot with the recommended amount of cooking liquid, lock the lid in position, and bring the pressure cooker up to pressure over high heat. Once you adjust the heat to stabilize the pressure (this is similar to preheating the oven), you *then* set the kitchen timer for the recommended cooking time. Got it?

✔ Undercook rather than overcook. When you're not entirely sure how long to cook something, undercooking is usually best. Mushy, overcooked food can't be salvaged, but undercooked food can be cooked a minute or two longer under pressure.

✔ Vegetarian recipes are marked with a tomato. Some otherwise meatless recipes may call for chicken broth. This can be replaced with vegetable stock and the recipe made vegetarian.

✔ All the recipes were developed and tested in the most popular 6-quart pressure cookers.

✔ Unless you're on a sodium-free diet, judiciously salt your food to taste as it cooks rather than at the end, except for beans and dried legumes, which should be salted only after they have cooked. I prefer to use kosher salt because it doesn't contain additives and therefore has a "cleaner" taste.

✔ Pepper should always be in the form of freshly ground black peppercorns for maximum flavor.

✔ I don't know what's worse: eating underseasoned or overseasoned food. Always taste a dish before serving and then season to taste with salt and pepper. If you happened to have a heavy hand with the salt, take a potato or two, peel and cut into ½-inch slices, and add it to the cooking liquid. The potato, as it cooks, will absorb a good deal of the saltiness.

✔ Oven temperatures are all in Fahrenheit.

✔ All eggs are large.

Part I

Stress-Free Cooking under Pressure

The 5th Wave   By Rich Tennant

In this part . . .

In Chapters 1 and 2, I tell you exactly what a pressure cooker is, how it works, and why you should use one every day when you cook! I also fill you in on how the pressure cooker has changed in the past 60 years, making it one of the fastest and safest methods of cooking. You find out what to expect in terms of new sizes and features, too.

Chapter 1

The Pressure Cooker: Fact versus Fiction

In This Chapter

▶ The maligning of a pot

▶ Dispelling the myths

▶ How safe are they really?

▶ The first pressure cookers

▶ Who's pressure cooking

▶ The benefits of owning a pressure cooker

▶ My recipes for success

A late Baby Boomer, I had heard about pressure cookers but had never really seen one in operation. As an undergraduate language major, I studied two years overseas at the University of Seville, in Spain, where I shared an apartment with three native Spanish students. Because I was the only one who knew the way around a kitchen, I became the appointed cook. In the kitchen of our furnished apartment was an 8-liter jiggler valve pressure cooker. Not sure what to do with it, and in all honesty somewhat apprehensive about using it, I at first put it away in the back of the cupboard.

A few weeks later, I went home with one of my roommates. The first thing I noticed as we walked into his family's apartment was a terrible racket coming from the kitchen. There on the stove sat a very noisy pot with a swirling valve that seemed to hiss and spit as it slowly spun around. After getting over my initial curiosity and eating the delicious stew that had been made in the pressure cooker, my curiosity got the better of me and I asked tons of questions about how to cook in the pressure cooker. Before I knew it, I was using the pressure cooker three to four times a week and spending about half the amount of time in the kitchen cooking as before!

One of the first things I did when I returned to New York was to buy an inexpensive aluminum pressure cooker. This was 1979, and no one I knew owned a pressure cooker or had ever used one. Nevertheless, I continued cooking under pressure as often as possible, amazing (and perhaps scaring) both family and friends, as back then only health food diehards and hippies were using pressure cookers — mostly to cook beans and grains. Other Americans were using a relatively new product at the time, something they called a slow cooker or crock pot (see *Slow Cookers For Dummies*, Hungry Minds, Inc.). Now, a little over 20 years later, close to 2 million pressure cookers are sold each year in this country!

I could not live without my collection of pressure cookers. In fact, I have at least seven or eight in my pantry on any given day, depending on whether or not my "loaners" have made it back home from friends who have come to see me as their very own personal housewares store. My pressure cookers have gotten me out of many a mealtime dilemma when 6:00 rolls around and I have yet to begin cooking. Depending on how many people I have to cook for on short notice, I have been known to have anywhere from three to four pressure cookers cooking away on my stove! Like most people today, I enjoy good food and like to cook, but am often hampered by tight schedules. The pressure cooker, however, enables me to get dinner on the table up to 70 percent faster than normal.

Dispelling Fears about Pressure Cookers

If ever there were a housewares product that was misunderstood and underutilized in American kitchens, it would, without a doubt, be the pressure cooker. Even though pressure cookers are enjoyed by tens of millions of home cooks worldwide without fear and crimination, the United States appears to be the last place on the earth where they are so underused, but ironically, so much needed.

Why is it, then, that while everyone else around the world relies on pressure cookers, many Americans think pressure cookers *dangerous* and *terrifying?* To understand why so many Americans are leery of using a pressure cooker, you need to understand something about the history of the pressure cooker and go back in time to the period just before and right after World War II.

A pre-WW II timesaver

Based on the success and popularity of 10-gallon home pressure canners, introduced in 1915, inventors began playing around with the idea of a smaller, more user-friendly pot that would be used on the stovetop to cook food in less time. One of the inventors was Alfred Vischer Jr., who after much trial and error introduced his safe-to-use Flex-Seal Speed Cooker in 1938 at a New York City trade show. This was the first time a safe, easy-to-use saucepan-sized pressure cooker was made available for consumer use. Department store buyers clamored to be the first in town to offer their customers this cookware wonder that afforded home cooks convenience and speed never before seen in the kitchen. Success led to competition, with other American and European manufacturers introducing their own brands and models of small, saucepan-sized pressure cookers.

Timing was critical, however, because just as pressure cookers were riding the wave of popularity, manufacturing came to a grinding halt as the United States entered World War II, bringing an end to all civilian production of cookware. This didn't hamper pressure cooker use, however. Faced with limited food supplies and rationing during the war, pressure cooker owners were encouraged by cookware manufacturers to be patriotic and share their pressure cookers with friends and family so that they too could enjoy the benefit of cooking cheap cuts of meat to tender perfection!

The untimely demise of the pressure cooker

At the end of the war, the success of the Vischer pressure cooker saucepan (as pressure cookers were then called) and post-war consumer demand inspired 85 competitive brands of U.S. pressure cooker saucepans to flood the market. While this may seem like a good thing, it was actually the beginning of the end of the pressure cooker boom, no pun intended!

Today's pressure cookers are safe

Even though some poorly designed and postwar-manufactured American-made pressure cookers did indeed explode and rupture, many food-spewing incidents can be attributed to people not reading the instructions or not knowing how to use their pressure cookers properly.

While today's new and improved pressure cookers can't be opened while cooking under pressure, this was not the case with the earlier units. Way too many times, an unsuspecting husband would want to get a peek at what was cooking for dinner and would remove the cover from a pressure cooker under pressure, causing an eruption of hot food. As Chapter 2 explains, this would be impossible today unless you were using a vintage model, because the new pressure cookers have safety features that make it impossible to remove the lid as long as there is an iota of pressure still inside.

With so many models to choose from, steep competition caused prices to drop, ultimately affecting the integrity and quality of the products. The all-too-familiar pressure cooker horror stories that we hear over and over again date from this period — the late 1940s through the early 1950s. Some U.S. manufacturers began to produce inferior-quality pressure cooker saucepans, and cooks were unhappy with the results. What once was the relatively safe pressure cooker, the home cook's friend, was now exploding and rupturing, spewing hot food all over clean kitchens. One by one, companies began to drop out of the business, with only those dedicated to the pressure cooker's development remaining in operation. The damage was done, however, and the pressure cooker's fate seemingly sealed! It took close to 50 years for American consumers to even consider cooking with a pressure cooker again.

Design changes mean a safer product as well as convenience

While America was getting on with life after the war, Europe was re-building, literally from the ground up. Civil production of most housewares items would not commence until the 1950s. Fortunately for us though, our European counterparts continued using their old, pre-war pressure cookers after the war. With rapidly growing post-war families and lifestyle changes due to advances in technology, European housewives were concerned with providing their families with traditional home-cooked meals in a relatively short time. Due to this demand and an ongoing interest in pressure cooking, major European manufacturers did not delay in improving the basic concept by developing new designs and incorporating improved safety features. (I talk about these features in Chapter 2.). We too would ultimately benefit from these improvements and advances when major European housewares manufacturers began to ship pressure cookers to the U.S. in the late 1980s and early 1990s.

Looking at the Benefits of Owning and Using a Pressure Cooker

If asked to give a one-word reason why I own and use a pressure cooker, my answer would be "fast." Or perhaps "convenient." No, most definitely "fast," and, well, also "delicious" and "healthy" too, since so many nutrients and vitamins are saved when food is cooked in a pressure cooker. Using a pressure cooker helps me produce fast, convenient, delicious, and nutritious food! I guess I'd be hard-pressed to use only a single adjective. For such a simple product, pressure cookers provide an awful lot for the buck! Let me tell you why.

Fast!

Pressure cookers use a combination of pressure and intense high heat from the built-up, trapped steam in order to cook food 38 degrees hotter than in a conventional saucepan or skillet. By doing so, they cut down on cooking time by up to 70 percent. If given the option of spending, say, 30 minutes cooking or an hour and a half, which would you choose? Easy answer, huh? Then why aren't you using your pressure cooker each and every day?

Because a pressure cooker cooks up to 70 percent faster, you also save on energy. Check out how much time you can save with just a few of the popular foods I've listed in Table 1-1:

Table 1-1	Cooking Time Comparisons: Pressure Cooker Method versus Traditional Cooking Method		
Food	*Pressure Cooker (in minutes)*	*Traditional Time (in minutes)*	*Savings (in minutes & percentage faster)*
Mashed potatoes	17	35	18 / 51%
Chicken soup	29	55	26 / 48%
Italian meat sauce	55	90	45 / 39%
Refried beans	30	135	105 / 78%
Sauerbraten (a type of marinated, German pot roast)	80	1800	1720 / 96%

Convenient!

Unlike microwaves and other new, fast-cooking gadgets, pressure cookers do not take up any counter space, nor do they require any special or expensive equipment. All you need is your gas or electric stove (including halogen and even glass cooktops, too) and a kitchen timer.

You can use your pressure cooker to make almost any conceivable type of food, as long as you prepare it with some liquid to create steam and pressure.

Pressure cookers are also energy efficient. Because they cook up to 70 percent faster and are on the stove for a much shorter period, by using them you ultimately reap the rewards of lower energy costs. Moreover, because all the hot steam stays in the pot while the food cooks, using your pressure cooker keeps your kitchen cooler in the summer — thus reducing your need for fans or air conditioning — than using conventional saucepans and skillets to simmer your food. Just be sure to release the steam under a ventilator hood so that the hot steam is vented to the outside.

Cooking in a pressure cooker is also cleaner than using a conventional saucepan or skillet. First, because the pressure cooker lid is locked in place, you eliminate the possibility of splattering cooking liquids all over the stove and surrounding areas. Secondly, when steam is emitted from a bubbling pot, it eventually settles on your stove and counters, leaving behind starch and mineral deposits. Because the steam is trapped in the pressure cooker, so are the starch and minerals.

Delicious!

Even though a pressure cooker cooks up to 70 percent faster than conventional cooking methods, you are basically cooking the food in the same way, building on flavor and appearance as you go along by sautéing and browning and then finishing the dish under pressure so that it cooks thoroughly. The resulting food is cooked to perfection and tasty, too! And why shouldn't it be? This is scratch cooking, after all, just sped up by 70 percent!

Healthy!

At the risk of showing my age, I'll ask this question: Do you remember a television commercial from years back for grape jelly that was cooked in a device that looked like a copper still? The gist of the commercial was that all the natural goodness was trapped in the copper tubes to keep in all the good flavor. Guess what? They were right, plus, the jelly probably had more nutrients in it, too!

Studies performed at the Analytic Chemical Laboratory at the Agronomic National Institute in Paris, France, show that valuable minerals and vitamins normally wash out and are poured down the drain when foods are cooked in conventional saucepans of water. These vitamins and minerals are retained at a much higher degree when steamed or cooked in a pressure cooker.

Because steam replaces the air space in the pot not occupied by food, foods do not oxidize and change color as quickly. Furthermore, the longer food is cooked, the more color and flavor it loses. That's why green veggies come out greener and carrots stay brighter when cooked in a pressure cooker, not to mention their more intense flavor!

Using your pressure cooker may also help you to avoid food poisoning. All too often, we hear of outbreaks of illness related to food contamination. Food poisoning is avoidable, however, especially when you're in control of your kitchen. I go over some of the safe cooking practices you should follow every day in Chapter 11. Nevertheless, you should know that because your pressure cooker cooks under pressure between 220 and 250 degrees, most harmful bacteria is killed off when meat is cooked until done (see Table 1-2).

Table 1-2	Cooking Temperatures of Commonly Prepared Foods
Food	*Safe Internal Cooking Temperature*
Ground meat	
Turkey/Chicken	165°
Beef, veal, lamb, or pork	160°
Fresh beef	
Medium	160°
Well done	170°
Fresh lamb	
Medium	160°
Well done	170°
Fresh pork	
Medium	160°
Well done	170°
Poultry	
Chicken	180°
Turkey	180°

My Recipes for Success, Not to Mention Fabulous-Tasting Food, Too!

As you read Chapter 3, you'll see that in addition to being fast, pressure cookers are easy to use. When given the opportunity to cook something in a saucepan or one of my pressure cookers, I always weigh my options to see how much time I'll save and then take it from there.

The best way to begin using your pressure cooker is to leave it out on the stovetop. This way, you'll be sure to see it when it comes time to cook. I can assure you that the more you use it and see how much time you save, the more cooking you'll do with it.

Over the years, I have been converting traditional recipes for use in the pressure cooker with excellent results. It's really quite easy to do, especially once you understand how a pressure cooker works. I give you all kinds of pointers and some sample converted recipes in Chapter 4.

Some older people may think of mushy, overcooked food when they remember the foods that their mothers made in their pressure cookers. This certainly does not have to be the case with today's models, because they are easier to use and much more accurate. To make things even easier for you, I share with you throughout this book all the tips and secrets I've learned over the years to making great food in almost no time at all. For the most part, the recipes are simple and are made with fresh ingredients available at your local grocery store.

If you've never used a pressure cooker before, go to Chapter 2 to find out how it works and get instructions on how to use it for the very first time. Then come back here.

To get you started, I've chosen one of my favorite soups, lentils with pasta. If you are new to the world of pressure cookers, this is a good place to start because I cover most of the things I like to do with my pressure cooker.

You begin by cooking the onion and garlic in some olive oil until soft. They add great flavor to the soup. Next, you add some diced carrots, celery, and tomatoes. You cook them only briefly to soften them a bit and draw out some flavor. Then you add the lentils, one of my favorite dried legumes, some water, and spices. You cover the pressure cooker and bring it to high pressure, and in about 10 minutes, the soup will be cooked to perfection, ready for the addition of some cooked pasta and a sprinkling of grated Pecorino Romano cheese! I hope that I've tempted you.

○ My Favorite Lentil Soup with Pasta

Lentils are a powerhouse of nutrition, containing almost as much protein as meat. Available in different varieties, the most common is the flat, brown lentil sold at supermarkets everywhere. One of my favorites, the smaller, plumper dark green or Puy lentil, is worth searching out and can be found at some health food and specialty food stores.

Preparation time: *10 minutes*

Cooking time: *4 minutes*

Yield: *4 servings*

2 tablespoons olive oil

1 medium onion, chopped

6 cloves garlic, crushed

2 carrots, peeled and diced

2 stalks celery, diced

2 whole plum tomatoes, fresh or canned, coarsely chopped

½ teaspoon dried oregano

Salt and freshly ground black pepper to taste

2 cups lentils, picked over, rinsed under cold water, and drained

6 cups water

1 cup small tubular pasta like ditalini or tubetti

Extra-virgin olive oil and grated Pecorino Romano or Parmesan cheese for garnish

1 Heat the olive oil in the pressure cooker over medium-high heat. Add the onion and garlic. Cook until the onion is soft. Add the carrots, celery, tomatoes, oregano, salt, and black pepper. Cook for 2 minutes. Add the lentils and water. Stir well.

2 Cover and bring to high pressure over high heat. Lower heat to stabilize pressure. Cook for 10 minutes. Meanwhile, cook the pasta according to package directions, until *al dente*.

3 Remove from the heat. Release the pressure with a Quick Release Method (see Chapter 2).

4 Open and remove the cover. Taste the lentils. If they're still hard, return to Step 2 and cook for an additional 1 to 3 minutes, or until tender.

5 Add the cooked pasta. Taste and adjust for salt and black pepper.

6 Drizzle each serving with some extra-virgin olive oil. Serve with the grated cheese.

Per serving: *Calories 495 (From Fat 77); Fat 9g (Saturated 1g); Cholesterol 0mg; Sodium 201mg; Carbohydrate 81g (Dietary Fiber 23g); Protein 28g. Analysis does not include olive oil and cheese.*

Chapter 2

How Your Pressure Cooker Works

● ●

In This Chapter

▶ Becoming acquainted with your pressure cooker

▶ Using and taking care of your pressure cooker

▶ Releasing the steam

▶ Testing your pressure cooker

● ●

The pressure cooker has come a long way from its early days when it resembled a cast-iron cannon ball and was heated in the hot cinders of the hearth until the cook "guessed" that the food was done (back in the days of our great-great grandparents!). It's different even from what it looked like a short seventy-five years ago when it was made from die-cast metal. Aside from being cosmetically different, today's stamped aluminum or stainless steel pressure cooker has at least three safety valves, making it the safest it's ever been.

If you've never used a pressure cooker before, or if you have but plan to start using one of the new and improved versions, carefully read the following information. I tell you everything you ever wanted to know about how this kitchen wonder works, and what to expect along the way as it does its thing.

Understanding How Your Pressure Cooker Works

With the exception of oil and fat, all liquids that contain water boil at 212 degrees Fahrenheit. When water boils, steam, which is hotter than boiling water, is produced.

For a moment, imagine a pot of boiling water that's producing steam. Cover the pot and close the cover in such a way so that the pot is sealed and the steam can't escape. As long as the liquid boils, the trapped steam continues to increase, eventually condensing with nowhere to go and building up inside the pot. The pressure of this trapped steam can be measured in pounds per square inch, which is also known as *psi*.

Now pretend that you have a 1-x-1-inch cube, and you're applying approximately 10 to 13 pounds of *force,* or pressure, on all six sides of the cube. With the combined heat and pressure, the cube (or food, in this case) starts to break down, or cook, which is exactly what happens when you prepare food in a pressure cooker. The combined heat and pressure also increase the cooking temperature by approximately 38 degrees. The combination of high heat and pressure can speed up the cooking process by as much as 70 percent. See Figure 2-1 for an illustration of cooking under pressure.

Figure 2-1:
Maximum capacity for filling the pressure cooker.

The Sum of the Parts

Pressure cookers are deceptively quite simple looking. When you consider that they consist of only four main components, it's pretty amazing that you can cook such delicious food, so quickly, in such a simple product. But don't be fooled. Each part plays an important role in getting the job done! The most important ones that you'll need to concern yourself with, are the following: the pot and cover with their plastic handles, the rubber gasket, and the different types of pressure regulator valves used on the three different types of pressure cookers made and sold today.

The pot and cover

The two main components of the pressure cooker are the pot and cover. Originally made from die-cast metal, pressure cookers have been made of stamped metal ever since this process was introduced in France in the 1950's. Today's stamped aluminum or stainless steel (usually high quality, 18/10 stainless) pressure cookers, are usually sold in a variety of sizes ranging from 4 to 8 quarts. The most commonly offered size is 6 quarts. This is the size that I use most often because it can easily accommodate a recipe that makes 4 to 8 servings.

Whether you purchase and use an aluminum or stainless steel pressure cooker is up to you. Aluminum is usually less expensive. However, the way I look at it, because I use my pressure cooker almost each and every day, I prefer a heavier, stainless steel model.

Why? Because most stainless steel pressure cookers have a thick three-ply plate attached to the bottom of the pot that comes in direct contact with the burner. Comprised of a sheet of aluminum or copper sandwiched between two sheets of stainless steel, this plate evenly distributes heat, eliminating hot or cold spots on the cooking surface. Because I like to sauté and brown in the same pressure cooker pot before cooking under pressure, I prefer a heavy-bottomed pot for even cooking. Also, the heavier the bottom, the less likely the food will stick and burn when cooking under pressure. Some less expensive aluminum pressure cookers have thin metal bottoms which increase the risk of food sticking and burning over high heat as the pressure cooker is brought up to pressure.

There are usually two heat-resistant plastic handles on the pressure cooker pot and two matching handles on the cover. Some pressure cookers have two short handles, while others may have a short handle on one end and a longer one on the opposite end. The handles are important for two reasons:

- Pressure cooker pots are heavy. A 6-quart stainless steel pot can weigh about 7 to 8 pounds empty; add some cooking liquid and food, and that pot gets awfully heavy mighty fast. The handles, therefore, make it easier to move the pressure cooker from the countertop to the burner.

- If you look at the underside of a pressure cooker cover and the top of the pot, you'll see a jar-like locking mechanism for closing and sealing the pressure cooker. When the pressure cooker is closed properly, the top handles on the cover line up with the bottom handles on the pot. Some pressure cooker cover handles also have a locking mechanism incorporated in the handle that has to be activated in order to lock the cover in place. Others self-lock when the cover is turned and locked in position.

Regardless of the design, pressure cookers today, unlike the ones back in the '40s and '50s, can't be opened until the pressure has dropped to zero psi. This is an important safety feature. Early model pressure cookers, for the most part, didn't explode. People opened them under pressure with food flying out and all over the kitchen! Fortunately for us, this can no longer happen. If you happen to have one of those older models, save it as a conversation piece. They're no longer meant for cooking!

Some of the most important parts of the pressure cooker are found on or under the cover. These include the rubber gasket and the pressure regulator and safety valves, discussed later in this section.

The ever-important rubber gasket

An important feature invented by Alfred Vischer, Jr. and incorporated in his 1938 Flex-Seal Speed Cooker (see Chapter 1) was the rubber seal or gasket. The seal creates an air- and steam-tight seal when the cover is locked in place. All pressure cookers must have this feature because without it they don't work.

Here's why. Because metal expands when heated, the rubber gasket allows for a constant tight seal between the cover and the pot. By having this constant seal, air cannot get into the pressure cooker. The steam that is created by the boiling cooking liquid is trapped inside the sealed pot and builds into pressure, which will ultimately cook the food up to 70 percent faster than if using a regular pot and cover.

In order to perform as required, the gasket must be clean and flexible. Over the course of time, it can dry out and harden, losing its elasticity. If that happens, replace the gasket immediately. Make a habit of checking the gasket each time you use your pressure cooker. Most manufacturers suggest that the gasket be replaced at least once a year. Never use your pressure cooker without the rubber gasket properly positioned. Don't use a damaged gasket because the cover will not lock into place properly and/or steam will not build up and may even escape.

Relying on the almighty valve!

In much the same way that electric appliances have on/off switches and temperature controls or settings, pressure cookers have pressure-regulator valves that allow you to control the amount of pressure inside the closed pot. Some of these valves have been around for decades; others are new and quite innovative. Basically, there are 3 types of pressure cookers; a pressure cooker's type is determined by the kind of valve it has. Figure 2-2 shows the three basic types of pressure cookers: jiggler valve, developed-weight valve, and spring valve.

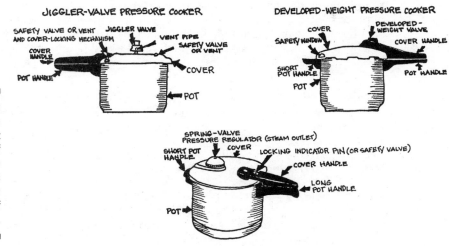

Figure 2-2:
Three different types of pressure cookers based on their kind of valves.

It's rock 'n' roll regulator time!: The jiggler valve

The jiggler valve is one of the oldest pressure-regulator methods around. People who recall that old, noisy pressure cooker sitting on top of their stove are thinking about the jiggler-valve type of pressure cooker (see the jiggler-valve pressure cooker in Figure 2-2).

The jiggler valve is a round, metal weight that sits on top of a thin metal tube, or vent pipe, in the center of the cover of some pressure cooker models. As pressure builds inside the pressure cooker, steam comes out through the vent pipe, causing that metal weight to rock back and forth and slowly turn. As pressure increases, so does the movement of the jiggler valve. In fact, the only method you have for figuring out the approximate level of pressure you're cooking with is one of trial and error. Exceed pressure, and the infamous jiggler valve hisses and spits steam and condensation at you with no mercy.

Today's jiggler-valve pressure cooker really hasn't changed too much since its introduction. It has some additional safety features, like not being able to remove the cover while under pressure. Unlike the earlier ones made from die-cast metal, today's versions are made from stamped aluminum, or in some cases, stainless steel.

The heavyweight: The developed-weight valve

A takeoff of the jiggler valve is the developed-weight valve (see the developed-weight pressure cooker in Figure 2-2). This pressure regulator valve is positioned on the vent pipe (the exact location of the vent pipe depends on the brand and model, although most are located on the cover handle) and locked in place by the user. When pressure is achieved, the weight rises up ever so slightly, and steam is emitted, indicating to the user that maximum pressure has been reached and that the moment has arrived to adjust the burner heat to a level low enough to maintain pressure.

It's all in the turn of the dial: Spring-valve pressure regulators

Over the course of time, manufacturers have devised easier ways to regulate pressure, the best of which is the spring-valve pressure regulator.

The design of the spring-valve pressure regulator is different from brand to brand. The following are two common examples:

✔ One type, as illustrated by the spring-valve pressure cooker in Figure 2-2, consists of a plastic dial that's located on top of the cover. Inside or under the removable dial is a spring mechanism. If you gently press down on the dial, you can feel the spring action. The dial usually has numerical settings and a burst-of-steam symbol that allow you to choose the level of pressure you want, as well as release pressure after cooking. The following gives a detailed description:

  • **Setting 0:** Releases the dial, allowing you to remove the cover for cleaning.

  • **Setting 1:** Used for low pressure (10 psi). Perfect for cooking soft foods, such as berries or fish, so they retain their shape.

  • **Setting 2:** Works for high pressure (13 to 15 psi, depending on brand and model). This is the setting I use most frequently when cooking under pressure.

  • **Steam:** Used to release pressure immediately after cooking.

✔ Another type of spring-valve pressure regulator consists of a plastic or metal rod that's built into the cover and rises as pressure builds in the pressure cooker. The spring-regulated rods indicate the level of pressure reached either by color and/or height. Some models also have a pressure selector switch built into the handle that allows you to select a level of pressure such as low (10 psi), medium (13 psi), or high (15 psi).

Hearing lots of hissing? It's the safety valves!

Once the cover is positioned on the pressure cooker and locked in place, the pressure cooker can be heated and brought up to maximum pressure over high heat. Steam pressure will gradually build up. Excess steam will begin to come out of the pressure regulator valve, and an audible hissing sound will be heard. These things happen with all pressure cookers, regardless of the type of pressure regulator valve.

If the burner heat is not adjusted and lowered, steam will continue to come out as a safety feature. As pressure continues to build, the other safety valves will also activate. All pressure cookers have at least three safety valves. Their function is to permit excess pressure to escape if too much pressure builds up because of one or more of the following reasons:

- ✔ The heat is too high, creating too much steam.
- ✔ A pressure regulator valve is malfunctioning or obstructed.
- ✔ The pressure cooker is overfilled.

Although every manufacturer refers to these valves by different names, for the most part they're very similar in operation. Basically, by making so much racket, the pressure cooker is reminding you to lower the burner heat to a simmer.

So where are these safety valves located? In addition to the pressure regulator valve, another safety valve is usually located in the cover. This valve may be as simple as a rubber stopper or plug in a juggler valve-type pressure cooker, or as sophisticated as a metal lug-nut-type valve. In addition, depending on the design of the pressure cooker, some type of safety valve is usually located in the cover handle, as well as a cutout in the cover rim that allows for expansion of the rubber gasket under extreme, excess pressure. Together, all these safety valves provide the user with a pressure cooker that is safer to use than ever before. Nevertheless, all the valves must be kept unobstructed and clear of any food buildup if they are to work properly.

Guidelines for Easy Pressure Cooking

As with any appliance or gadget, you have some basic, fundamental rules to follow to get the best results before and while you use your pressure cooker.

As you pressure cook, always remember the following points:

- ✔ **Because food, especially liquid, boils harder and faster under pressure, it has a tendency to increase in volume.** For this reason, never fill the pressure cooker more than half full with food or two-thirds full with liquid when making soups or sauces. Most pressure cookers have a two-thirds mark stamped on the inside of the pot, eliminating any guesswork. (See Chapter 3 for more details).

Never pack food down into the pressure cooker because that defeats the purpose of fast cooking by inhibiting the very hot steam from circulating among the food.

✔ **Maximize flavor by browning meat and poultry directly in the pressure cooker.** When food is cooked quickly over high heat in a small amount of fat, like canola or olive oil, it browns. The natural sugar found in food caramelizes in the hot fat, giving the food great color, as well as developing intense flavor. I therefore always brown or sauté meat, poultry, chopped onions, carrots, celery, and at times, some hearty herbs like thyme or sage, to give the food I am preparing better flavor and ultimately texture.

✔ **When browning, you want the temperature to be hot enough to sear in the juices and flavor, but not burn the food.** So, when making My Favorite Beef Stew (see Chapter 8), I'm going to heat the oil in the pressure cooker pot over medium-high heat. When I think that the oil is hot enough, I'll add a piece or two of meat. If it sizzles without sputtering, I know that the oil is at the ideal temperature. I'll add about half of the meat and cook it evenly on all sides. If I add too much meat at once, the oil and pot will drop in temperature and the meat with simmer rather than brown. This is called cooking in batches. I'll deglaze the pan with some red wine before proceeding to cook under pressure. By deglazing, I'll be removing cooked-on particles of meat and onion as well as any cooked-on juices. This is what will make our stew so flavorful. The wine and tomatoes will also create the steam needed to cook under pressure.

Always brown with the cover off and usually over high or medium-high heat in order to sear the outer surface of the meat. Marinated foods should be well drained, and all meat and poultry should be patted dry before placing in the hot oil.

✔ **Never force the cover when closing it.** If the cover won't easily close and lock, remove it from the pressure cooker and make sure that the rubber gasket is properly positioned. The cover should sit squarely on the center of the pressure cooker before you try to close it.

If you force the cover closed, you may never get your pressure cooker open again!

Some covers lock in place by being positioned on the pressure cooker and turned clockwise. These units usually have an arrow or some type of indicator mark on the cover that enables you to line it up in the right position. Simply place the cover on the pressure cooker with the indicator mark lined up with the long pot handle. Making sure that the cover is sitting flush to the pot, carefully turn clockwise. Because of the tight fit of the rubber seal gasket, some covers may offer more resistance than others when you're closing the pressure cooker. Regardless, never force the cover shut because that is an indication that it probably isn't lined up properly and will be very difficult, if not impossible, to reopen.

Some pressure cookers have a self-locking cover mechanism. You simply position the cover on the pressure cooker in accordance with the manufacturer's instructions and lock it in place.

✔ **The countdown time for cooking begins when the pressure cooker reaches the level of pressure chosen and not before. Pressure is rated in psi, or pounds per square inch. The higher the pressure, the hotter the food is cooking (see Table 2-1).**

✔ **Because pressure cookers cook up to three times faster than conventional cooking methods, food can overcook!** Carefully follow cooking times when using a pressure cooker recipe or a suggested cooking times chart. If you're uncertain about the exact time to cook something, undercook it. Undercooked food can easily be cooked under pressure an additional minute or two, whereas overcooked food usually becomes purée!

Table 2-1	Temperature-Pressure Ratios	
Pressure Level	_Cooking Temperature_	_Pressure Level_
High pressure	250 degrees	13–15 psi
Medium pressure	235 degrees	10 psi
Low pressure	220 degrees	3 psi

Letting Off Some Steam

Unless otherwise indicated in a recipe, pressure should always be released immediately after the required length of cooking time to prevent overcooking. There are three methods to release the steam, the natural method and two quick-release methods.

When releasing pressure, always choose the appropriate method for your model pressure cooker or in accordance with the recipe's instructions.

Natural release method

This method can be used with all types of pressure cookers but is specifically used for recipes such as pot roast or stocks and broth. Such foods benefit by the additional cooking time in the closed pot: pot roast becomes more tender; stock becomes more flavorful.

1. **After cooking for the prescribed length of time, remove the pressure cooker from the burner and let it cool to room temperature.**

   As it cools, the pressure diminishes and eventually drops completely. The exact amount of time depends on how full the pressure cooker is.

   If using a jiggler-valve or weighted-valve pressure cooker, you can tell that the pressure was released when you can touch or remove the valve and it no longer makes any noise.

   Pressure has been released in a spring-valve pressure cooker when the pressure indicator pin drops all the way.

2. **Open the pressure cooker.**

Use only the natural release method when cooking large, tough cuts of meat that will not break down and get mushy and that can only benefit from the additional cooking time, or when making stock or broth when the solids (vegetables, poultry, meat, and so on) will be discarded.

Quick-release methods

The next two methods are *quick-release methods*. These are the two most commonly used ways of releasing pressure. The method you use is determined by the model of pressure cooker you have, so check your manufacturer's instructions.

Cold water release method

This is the method to use if you have a jiggler valve, weighted valve, or spring-regulated valve pressure cooker *without* a pressure selector.

1. **When finished cooking, remove the pressure cooker from the stove using potholders to grab the two handles, and place it in the sink.**

2. **Run cold water over the top side of the pressure cooker until all the pressure has been released.**

   If using a jiggler-valve or weighted-valve pressure cooker, you can tell that the pressure was released when you can touch or remove the valve and it no longer makes any noise.

   Pressure has been released in a spring-valve pressure cooker when the pressure indicator pin drops all the way.

3. **Open the pressure cooker when all the pressure has been released.**

Automatic release method

Use this method to release pressure after cooking, if your pressure cooker has a pressure selector with steam release, usually indicated by a burst of steam symbol.

1. **Carefully turn or push the pressure selector to the steam setting to release the pressure.**

   The pressure cooker automatically and safely releases all the built-up steam through the spring regulator valve.

   Pressure has been released when the pressure indicator pin drops all the way.

   Open the pressure cooker when all the pressure has been released.

In the event you are unable to open the cover, repeat the cold water release method again since there still may be some remaining pressure.

Doing a Trial Run

The easiest way to get the feel for how to use a pressure cooker is by putting it through a test run and heating some water under pressure before you begin cooking any food.

Follow these steps for heating water:

1. **Fill the pressure cooker pot with 2 cups of water.**

2. **Cover the pot.**

   Look for the two arrows or triangles that are engraved in the top of the cover. Place the cover on the pot, matching the arrows with the long pot handle. Turn clockwise until the cover and long pot handles line up together and you hear a click. If your pressure cooker is not shown in Figure 2-2, then check the owner's manual for instructions.

   Before positioning and locking the cover in place, always check the gasket to make sure that it's in good condition. Position it properly on the underside of the cover. Always check the owner's manual to see if the gasket has to be positioned in a specific fashion or location, since some gaskets have small cutouts or openings which must be lined up in order for the pressure cooker to work properly.

   Never force the cover when turning it to close. It should sit level on top of the pressure cooker and turn without much resistance. If you should encounter difficulties, please refer to Chapter 11.

If you don't hear a click when closing the pressure cooker, the cover isn't locked and won't operate properly. In that case, inspect the gasket, cover, and pressure cooker pot for possible damage.

3. **For a jiggler valve or developed-weight valve pressure cooker, place the weighted valve on the vent pipe. If you have a spring-valve pressure cooker and it has a pressure selector, set the regulator for the level of pressure desired, in this case high.**

4. **Place the pressure cooker on the stove and bring the water to a boil over high heat.**

   As the water boils, steam is produced.

   If your pressure cooker is the jiggler-valve type, the jiggler valve will slowly begin to turn and rock as steam pressure builds up. With the weighted valve type, the valve will raise slightly.

   The mode of operation with spring-valve pressure regulators is even more diverse: Some have a pressure indicator pin that rises up until it's level with the top of the cover. Others only have a pressure regulator valve that rises higher than the cover itself. Regardless, once they're up, this means that your pressure cooker has reached the level of pressure you choose to cook with.

5. **Lower the burner heat to simmer.**

   The pressure cooker is now cooking under pressure, which is when you start to clock the cook-down time.

If you don't own a digital kitchen timer, now is the time to purchase one. Available in the gadget section of most housewares stores and supermarkets, digital timers allow you to control the exact cooking time without any guesswork. If your stove has a digital timer, you can use that as well.

Make sure to watch for the following things:

- ✔ After you raise the heat to high, the pressure cooker will eventually start to hiss at you as it releases excess steam and pressure through the pressure selector. The pressure cooker is signaling you that it has reached the level of pressure you selected and it's time for you to immediately lower the burner heat to a low setting, which on my gas range is a simmer.

- ✔ If the pressure cooker is still pretty noisy after lowering the heat (with the exception of the jiggler and weighted valve versions, which normally operate with a certain amount of noise), turn the spring-valve pressure-regulator to the steam release setting for a couple seconds to release some of the excess pressure. Things should now be stabilized, the pressure cooker almost quiet, and hardly any steam coming out of the pressure regulator.

✔ If the jiggler valve slows down or stops spinning or if the weighted valve or indicator pin begins to lower while you're cooking, raise the burner heat slightly so the valves remain operational.

To remove the cover after cooking, follow these steps:

1. **Turn off the burner heat and remove the pressure cooker from the stove.**

2. **If using a jiggler valve, weighted valve-type pressure cooker or a spring regulator valve pressure cooker without a pressure selector switch, remove the pressure cooker from the stove and place in the sink. Run cold water over the top side of the pressure cooker until all the pressure has been released. For a spring regulator valve pressure cooker with a pressure selector, turn the selector to the steam setting to release the pressure.**

   The pressure cooker automatically and safely releases all the built-up steam. You will be able to open and remove the cover only when all the steam has been released.

   As long as any pressure remains in the pot, a safety-locking valve kicks in and makes removing the cover impossible.

3. **Unlock the cover.**

What could be easier? Let's start cooking!

Part II

Making the Best and Safest Use of Your Pressure Cooker

The 5th Wave By Rich Tennant

"Let's try to remember to use the safety pressure release valve the next time we're cooking a turkey in the pressure cooker."

In this part . . .

Here is where I reveal some of the finer points concerning the use and care of pressure cookers. I also share with you some of the tricks I've learned along the way for getting the best results with the least amount of effort. You also discover how to convert your favorite recipes cooked using traditional methods into recipes for the pressure cooker.

Chapter 3

Pressure Cooker Basics from Start to Finish

· ·

In This Chapter

▶ Establishing a routine for pressure cooker use

▶ Discovering ways to cook in a pressure cooker

▶ Finding out about stop-and-go cooking

▶ Maintaining pressure

▶ Cleaning your pressure cooker

· ·

*I*n this chapter, I give you some pointers on things to look for every time you use your pressure cooker, as well as tips on how to maintain it in perfect working shape for optimum use day after day, year after year. If you haven't looked at Chapter 2 yet, you may find it helpful to read that information first, so that you're more familiar with the basic pressure cooker parts and techniques that I refer to in this chapter.

First Things First

The following five sections explain in detail the steps involved in this routine. Observing each of these steps will ensure many happy and successful hours of pressure cooking.

Keep it clean

Always wash the pressure cooker well after every use or if it hasn't been used for an extended period of time. Never leave any food or residue in or on the pot and cover. If you see something that doesn't look like it belongs there, wash it off. For more pointers on cleaning your pressure cooker, flip to the end of this chapter or see Chapter 11.

Everything in Its Place

Cooking under pressure means cooking quickly. Because events move along at a rapid pace when pressure cooking, I like to have all of my ingredients already prepped and ready for the pot even before I turn on the burner. *Mise en place* is French for "everything in its place" which is what I suggest you do when cooking under pressure. Have all your ingredients cleaned, cut up, and measured before you begin cooking. Doing so will make your time in the kitchen seem less stressed. In addition, you'll be less likely to wonder whether you forgot to add an ingredient because it will be set out right before you on the counter.

Also remember to remove the gasket from the cover and check to see that the gasket, the inner part of the cover, and the outer rim of the pot are clean. If these areas are clean, you reduce the risk that the cover will stick when you open the pressure cooker after cooking once the pressure has been released.

Remove and inspect the rubber sealing gasket or ring

The gasket is what makes the pressure cooker airtight so that it can maintain pressure. Every time you use the pressure cooker, make sure that the rubber gasket is still flexible and hasn't dried out.

I always check the gasket visually for any tears or cracks. Take the gasket in two hands, twist it into a figure 8, and stretch it. There should be some give. If not, or if you notice any signs that the gasket is dry or damaged, replace it immediately with a new gasket, obtainable from the manufacturer (see Appendix A for manufacturers' consumer assistance phone numbers).

Nothing is worse than preparing all the food for the pressure cooker and then discovering that the rubber gasket is damaged. I suggest that you do like I do, and check the gasket *before* you begin to cook.

After checking the gasket, put it back in the rim on the underside of the cover. The gasket must slide flatly under the rim. Some pressure-cooker gaskets have markings or cutouts that indicate where to position them.

Check the valves

Just as you would never drive a car with a leaking gas tank, you should never use a pressure cooker with leaks. Routinely check your pressure cooker for leaks as well as blockages in the safety valves. Each manufacturer's design varies, so check the owner's manual for the exact requirements for maintaining the safety valves in working order. The following are some of the things I look for:

- If your pressure cooker has a jiggler valve or developed weight with a vent pipe, stick a pipe cleaner or toothpick through the opening to make sure that the vent pipe is clean and not blocked. Also check the underside of the jiggler valve or weight and remove any caked-on food residue. Some of these pressure cookers have a rubber stopperlike valve on the top of the cover. Be sure that it is securely positioned and has not dried out. Others have a brass or steel nutlike valve on the underside of the cover. Make sure that no food or residue has collected in the center of the nut.

- If your pressure cooker has a spring valve, press or pull gently on the valve (depending on the design) to make sure that it moves without any resistance. Visually check any remaining valves on the underside of the cover. For the most part, these resemble brass or steel nutlike valves. Another place to look for valves is in the handle assemblies. Here, too, remove any caked-on food or food residue.

Fill the pressure cooker properly

Although steam weighs nothing, it does require space as it builds up. If you fill the pressure cooker with too much food or liquid, the steam and pressure will force the food or liquid up towards the cover and safety valves. As the pressure builds, food and liquid will be forced out through the valves, which is dangerous since food particles can become lodged in the valves!

On the other hand, if you use too little cooking liquid, the pressure cooker may never reach pressure. Here are a couple tips to help you:

- Never fill the pressure cooker more than two-thirds full.
- Always use at least 2 cups of cooking liquid to obtain maximum pressure output.

Look, listen, and smell

As the pressure cooker begins to do its job, keep your senses alert to what is happening.

✔ **Look** to see that the pressure regulator valve is operating properly and that the pressure cooker is not taking longer than the anticipated amount of time to reach pressure. A good ballpark amount of time is about 5 to 10 minutes.

If you happen to see condensation leaking from the cover onto the stove as the pressure cooker reaches or is cooking under pressure, you don't have an airtight seal or the pressure cooker was overfilled. Stop everything and do the following. Release any pressure in the pot, remove the cover, and check to make sure that the gasket is indeed there and that it was properly positioned and not damaged. Remove any excess food if filled more than two-thirds full.

✔ **Listen** to the pressure regulator valve as it talks to you. Jiggler valve pressure cookers are the nosiest kind there are. In order to cook under pressure, some steam and pressure have to come out of the vent pipe that the jiggler valve sits on; as it does, it makes a hissing sound. No sound, no pressure! The more sound the jiggler valve makes, the higher the level of pressure you're cooking at.

Weighted valve and spring valve pressure cookers should make noise only when the pressure cooker exceeds the level of pressure chosen for the recipe or food being cooked. For example, suppose that you choose to cook at low pressure and set the pressure cooker accordingly, either with a low pressure valve (weighted valve model) or by setting the spring valve on low. Once the pressure exceeds low, the excess pressure has to go somewhere. Slowly but surely, it is released through the pressure regulator valve and starts to make a racket. This is an essential safety feature. Basically, the pressure cooker is telling you, "Hey, you set me on low pressure, I got there, so why don't you lower the burner to a simmer and not make me sweat it out!"

✔ **Smell** (from a safe distance!) and you will notice that the steam coming out of the pressure release valve is odorless; rarely will you smell anything while cooking under pressure. Rest assured, however, that if you cook at temperatures way too high, the food will stick and eventually burn. The food will also stick and burn and the pot will scorch if you don't use enough liquid and it evaporates. Trust me. This is not a pretty sight!

Three Ways to Cook in a Pressure Cooker

There is more one than one way to cook food in a pressure cooker. You can do any of the following:

- ✔ Steam under pressure by using water and some sort of a steaming basket or tray. This technique is perfect for cooking farm-fresh vegetables and fresh lobster. You can also steam desserts such as cheesecake, puddings, and custards, which you would normally bake in the oven in a hot water bath — otherwise known as a *bain-marie*.

  If your pressure cooker has a metal steaming basket, you'll no longer end up with waterlogged veggies (Chapter 9), and you'll be able to create pressure-cooker-baked goodies like my cheesecake recipes in Chapter 10, and more. Fill the pressure cooker with 2 to 3 cups of water. Put the trivet in the pot and the steaming basket on top. Fill with vegetables or whatever food you want to steam. Then cover and cook under pressure for the recommended cooking time.

- ✔ Prepare foods under pressure that contain a lot of liquid, including some of my favorite soups that I'm going to share with you in Chapter 5. These recipes include a chunky Beef Barley Mushroom, and a very creamy, Louisiana Yam, both of which I prepare in a fraction of the time it would take using conventional methods.

- ✔ Make an endless variety of entree and side dishes like Sunday Pot Roast in Chapter 7 and My Favorite Beef Stew in Chapter 8, starting off as you normally would by browning or sautéing in the open pressure cooker first (see Chapters 2 and 8 for more information) and then finishing up the dish with a quick braise under pressure (see Chapter 7 for information on braising). This two-step cooking process is probably my favorite way to use the pressure cooker, especially when time is short and I need to get dinner on the table is less than an hour.

Deep-frying is a no-no

Do not deep-fry in a pressure cooker regardless of whether or not the cover is on. Oil is a flammable liquid that is rated by smoke point, or the temperature at which the oil will burst into flames. Because you have no way to gauge the internal temperature of the hot oil as it heats in a closed pressure cooker, you have no idea how hot it is. Oil that reaches or exceeds its smoke point combusts and bursts into flames. You don't want to remove the pressure cooker cover to find flames shooting out of the pot. If you want to deep-fry foods, invest in an electric deep-fryer or use a frying pan.

Stop-and-Go Cooking

Not all food needs to cook for the same length of time (see Chapter 4 for a table of recommended cooking times). So what happens when you're preparing a dish such as stew, which contains meat that needs to cook at least 20 minutes and vegetables that cook in less than half that time? If the vegetables are added at the beginning with the meat, you know that they will cook too much and become mushy. The only way to avoid this is to cook under pressure in steps, or — as I like to call it — *stop-and-go cooking*. To give you a better idea of what I mean, refer to the following two scenarios.

Scenario 1: The long and the short of it

Let's use My Favorite Beef Stew recipe in Chapter 8 as the first scenario example. To be fork-tender, stew meat needs to cook at least 20 minutes under pressure. The green beans, carrots, celery, and potatoes, collectively, need less than 10 minutes; the mushrooms need only 60 seconds. What's a cook to do? You have to group and cook the ingredients in stages, starting with the longest-cooking ingredients and finishing up with the shortest. Think of it in terms of steps.

1. **Cook the meat under pressure for 15 minutes. Then release the pressure using a quick-release method.**

2. **Add all the veggies, except the mushrooms, and cook them with the meat for 8 minutes. As the vegetables cook with the meat, a wonderful gravy is being made with all of the juices and the red wine. Once again, when it's done, we release the pressure using a quick-release method.**

3. **Add the mushrooms and cook them for 1 minute under pressure.**

All together, the meat cooked for 15 minutes, plus 8 minutes, plus another 1 minute, for a total of 24 minutes under pressure. The meat is fork-tender, having been cooked to perfection for the right amount of time; the faster cooking vegetables also cooked for the right amount of time, so they retained their shape and flavor. And because all the ingredients were cooked together, the stew gravy is amazingly flavorful.

Scenario 11: Soup versus stock

Another good example of how different cooking times affect the results of a dish is comparing chicken soup to chicken stock (see Chapter 5). Both recipes have very similar ingredients. How they are handled, however, determines the end result.

When I make chicken soup, I want to extract enough flavor from the chicken and the vegetables so that I have a good broth. I know that the chicken pieces need only about 15 minutes to cook, whereas small-cut veggies are done in under 5 minutes. Because I dislike dry, tasteless chicken and mushy vegetables, I have to cook them for different lengths of time by following these steps:

1. **To make the broth, first cook the chicken in salted water, under pressure, to completion in 15 minutes. So that the chicken doesn't overcook, release the pressure using a quick-release method.**

2. **After removing the cooked chicken, add the vegetables to the chicken broth and cook them for only 4 minutes under pressure. So that the veggies don't get mushy, release the pressure using a quick-release method.**

3. **Add some cooked noodles and the cooked chicken that you cut into chunks while the vegetables were cooking. The soup is now ready to serve.**

The broth has a rich taste of the chicken and vegetables that were cooked in it. The chicken is tender and juicy; the vegetables are cooked to perfection!

Although chicken stock is basically made from the same ingredients as chicken soup, the process and end result are different. The objective in making chicken stock to extract as much flavor from the chicken and vegetables as possible. To do so, I don't employ stop-and-go cooking. Instead, I cook all the ingredients together for the same amount of time until they're so soft that they're virtually tasteless. To make sure this happens, I remove the pressure cooker from the stove and I let the pressure release on its own by using the natural release method. You see, as long as there is any pressure left in the closed pot, whatever is inside continues cooking.

After pressure-cooking chicken stock, all of the flavor has been extracted from the chicken and vegetables and is now in the stock. I, therefore, usually discard the cooked chicken and vegetables after straining the cooking liquid.

The High and Low of It

When you cook with conventional cookware and bakeware, either on the stovetop or in the oven, you can always take a look at the food to see how it's coming along or whether it's done cooking. Because a pressure cooker is a sealed pot, you can't peek in without releasing pressure and stopping the whole cooking process. Timing is therefore of the utmost importance.

The whole idea of using a pressure cooker is to save time. In fact, food cooks up to 70 percent faster in a pressure cooker than most conventional methods. To get things going quickly, you always want to begin cooking over high heat. Once the pressure cooker reaches pressure, you need to lower the burner to a near simmer, or whatever it takes to maintain pressure without exceeding it.

But if the cover is locked in place how do you know when to lower the heat to start the countdown for cooking? That's easy — you set the timer once the pressure cooker reaches and maintains the level of pressure you've chosen. When you bake a cake in the oven, you always preheat the oven before baking, right? The same holds true when a pressure cooker is coming up to pressure. You bring it up to pressure over high heat. It's like preheating before you're ready to start cooking under pressure.

Telling whether you've reached high pressure

If you use a jiggler valve-type pressure cooker (see Chapter 2), you know that the pressure cooker is up to pressure when the jiggler valve is rocking 'n' rolling at an even pace and there is some hissing going on. Now's the time to lower the burner to a simmer or thereabouts and start the cooking count-down time.

With a developed-weight valve or a spring valve pressure cooker (see Chapter 2), you'll know that the pressure cooker has reached pressure when the weighted valve rises up or when the pressure regulator indicator is in the upright position. Wait until the pressure cooker begins to make just a bit of noise, and then lower the burner heat. Set the kitchen timer for the recommended cooking time, and you're on your way.

Maintaining pressure

You'll know that you've exceeded pressure when the pressure release valve and safety valves start to make a hissing noise. Basically, the pressure cooker is telling you to lower the burner heat. How you do it depends on the type of stove you have.

Gas stoves

If you cook on a gas stove, you already know that a simple turn of the burner knob one way causes the heat to go up immediately; turn it in the opposite direction, and it drops almost instantaneously.

So what are you waiting for? Turn down the heat, almost to a simmer, or until you are able to maintain pressure without exceeding it! You'll see within a minute or so that the pressure cooker will get quiet again as it is now content, being able to work as designed.

Element hopscotch

If you have an electric range, you know that, unlike gas stoves, turning the dial does not elicit an instant response from the element. Electric elements take longer than gas burners to react when you raise or lower the heat. This can be a problem when you cook with a pressure cooker. To overcome this problem, I suggest that you play "element hopscotch."

In simple terms, element hopscotch means that you cook on two elements: one set on high heat and one set on a lower setting, or whatever setting on your range that keeps water boiling at a simmer. Use the element set on high heat to heat the pressure cooker for browning or sautéing the food. You also use the high heat element to bring the pressure cooker up to pressure once the cover is in place and locked into position

After the pressure cooker reaches pressure, transfer the pressure cooker to the preheated element that is set on the lower setting. (***Note:*** Don't forget to turn off the high heat element after the transfer!) This element must be set low enough so that the pressure cooker doesn't exceed pressure. On the other hand, it has to be hot enough so that the pressure cooker can maintain the level of pressure it has reached without dropping. If not, the food may take longer to cook.

Now You're Cooking

After the pressure cooker reaches pressure, the burner heat is lowered, and the kitchen timer is set, the pressure cooker should be fine doing its own thing. For the most part, you can take a breather, but don't go too far from the kitchen. You need to be around in case the pressure cooker gets too hot and begins to exceed pressure. There's really no need to be alarmed if it does, however. If you happen to hear it making a racket, just lower the burner heat until it stops.

Is it done yet?

Remember to remove the pressure cooker from the burner heat and release the pressure when the kitchen timer rings. Use one of the quick-release methods discussed in Chapter 2 or use the natural release method.

Always choose the appropriate release method for the type of food you are making. Use the natural release method when preparing foods like large cuts of meat or stocks that will benefit from the additional cooking time as the pressure drops on its own. For all other foods, use a quick release method, described in Chapter 2.

After releasing the pressure and removing the cover (see the following section for safety tips), check to see that the food is cooked. If it's still hard, replace the cover and cook for an additional couple minutes under pressure.

Opening the pressure cooker safely

The food in the pressure cooker is extremely hot, so be careful opening and removing the cover. Hold the griplike handle on the pot with one hand and turn the cover counterclockwise by grasping and turning the cover handle. If you have a pressure cooker with a self-locking cover, check the owner's manual for information on how to open and close.

Regardless of the method you use to release the pressure, always remember the following when opening and removing the cover:

✔ Always place the pressure cooker on a heatproof, stable surface.

✔ Steam is hotter than boiling water and can cause serious burns. Avoid contact with hot steam when releasing pressure and removing the cover. If you use the automatic quick-release method (see Chapter 2), watch where your hands are in relation to where the steam comes out when pressure is released so that you don't burn them.

Be careful removing the cover as well. Even though there is no further pressure in the pressure cooker, the cooked food will be very hot, and some steam will be rising up out of the pressure cooker. To avoid getting burned, never hold your face over the pressure cooker as you remove the cover.

Keeping Your Pressure Cooker Squeaky Clean and Shiny

Clean and maintain your pressure cooker like any other good piece of quality cookware. By doing so, you will get many years of quick and easy-to-prepare meals out of it.

Before putting your pressure cooker away, clean it by following these steps:

1. **Remove the gasket from the cover and wash it separately by hand.**

2. **Wash the pressure cooker cover, pot, and gasket with a mild, liquid dishwashing soap and a nonabrasive sponge after each use. Rinse well under clean water.**

   Consult Chapter 11 if you have any problems getting your pressure cooker clean.

   Never immerse the cover in water because it may affect and damage the safety valves. Never wash the pressure cooker in the dishwasher. Food particles in the dishwasher recycling wash water or even dishwasher detergent can collect and clog the pressure regulator and/or safety valves.

3. **Towel dry all parts and properly reposition the rubber gasket under the cover.**

   Some gaskets have to be lined up a specific way. Make sure that you replace it correctly.

Some manufacturers suggest that the pressure regulator valve be disassembled and cleaned after each use. Check the manufacturer's instructional materials for further information.

For more cleaning tips, see Chapter 11.

Storing Your Pressure Cooker

Storing your pressure cooker properly is essential to maintaining its long and useful life. Here are some pointers on what *not* to do:

- Never store the pot with food inside. Doing so is inefficient since the pressure cooker would take up too much room in the refrigerator. Furthermore, the food may stain the interior surface or pick up off-flavors. Always clean and dry your pressure cooker thoroughly before putting it away.

- Never lock the cover in place because you can damage the rubber gasket seal or ring or, worse yet, not be able to reopen the pressure cooker due to moisture that can create an almost permanent seal.

The best way to store the cover is to place it upside down on the top of the pressure cooker. Never store the cover locked into position on the pot because doing so can damage the cover. Over an extended period of time, the rubber gasket can dry out and form a permanent bond with the pot and cover, making it nearly impossible to open the pressure cooker.

Help Is But a Phone Call Away

Although I have tried to anticipate and answer any questions or concerns that I think you may have, you may need to contact the pressure cooker manufacturer if you have specific questions about your pressure cooker. All the manufacturers have fully staffed customer service departments with trained representatives who are happy to answer your questions. A list of various pressure cooker manufacturers is given in Appendix A, along with their customer service phone numbers.

Chapter 4

From the Pot to the Pressure Cooker

Many people are reluctant to cook because they think they don't have the time to do it. If you use a pressure cooker, however, you don't need a lot of time. You'll be able to get a nutritious, home-cooked dinner ready after you come home from work instead of relying on take-out and processed foods. The great thing about this kitchen cooking wonder is that you can use it to cook just about anything. In fact, many great dishes cook up to 70 percent faster when prepared in a pressure cooker. With a couple of minor tweaks here and there, most recipes can be easily adapted to a pressure cooker. It's all a matter of knowing what works, how much, and for how long!

Naturally, some foods are better suited for the pressure cooker than others, and I share this information with you, as well as some tips on how to properly prepare the different ingredients and foods you'll be cooking under pressure. But before I do that, sit back and read the following section as I tell you, step-by-step, how I adapted one of my favorite, albeit time-consuming, recipes, for the pressure cooker.

Adapting Your Favorite Recipes for the Pressure Cooker

Understanding how your pressure cooker works is the first step to knowing how to adapt recipes. The second is knowing how long things take to cook under pressure and the order in which to cook them. Finding all this out really isn't as complicated as it may seem, and as you read further in this chapter, you'll get a better idea of what I'm talking about.

One way to adapt a traditional recipe is to find a similar pressure cooker recipe and use it as your guide. For example, suppose that you want to make your favorite beef stew recipe. I suggest that you refer to My Favorite Beef Stew in Chapter 8. First, you brown the meat in batches in hot oil in the pressure cooker to sear in the juices and flavor. Next, you cook some onion in the same oil. Once the onions are soft, add some wine and then tomatoes to deglaze the bottom of the pot by dissolving the cooked-on juices and any cooked-on particles. You're now ready to cook the meat under pressure. When the meat is almost done, you add the vegetables. You don't add them at the beginning because if you do, they'll overcook and come out mushy. By following these same steps and using my recipe cooking times as a guide, you can adapt your beef stew recipe to the pressure cooker.

For successful results, never lose sight of the fact that pressure cookers cook differently than other conventional cooking methods in terms of timing, ingredients, and the amount of liquids. I discuss these practical points in the following sections.

Determining Cooking Times

When you cook in an open pot, you can easily taste and test the food as it cooks to determine when it's done. But you can't do this with a pressure cooker. To cook under pressure, the cover must be locked in place, meaning that you can't sample the food quite as often during the cooking process. The only way to physically test something is to remove the pressure cooker from the heat, release the pressure, and remove the cover.

If you don't test the food soon enough, the food can overcook. With the exception of tough cuts of meat, overcooked food can become mush in a matter of seconds. Therefore, undercooking is always better than overcooking. If food needs to be cooked longer, you can always replace the cover, bring the pressure cooker back up to pressure, and continue cooking for another minute or two until the food is done.

The easiest way to determine cooking times is to refer to the cooking times charts found in most of the recipe chapters. You can find complete charts for grains, dried beans and legumes, meat, poultry, vegetables, and fruits. Table 4-1 is an abbreviated pressure cooker cooking times chart for the most commonly prepared foods. The cooking times in the table begin when the pressure cooker reaches *high pressure*. Always start with the shortest cooking time; you can always continue cooking under pressure for an additional couple minutes until the desired texture is reached.

All cooking times are at best approximations and should be considered a general guideline. Not all types of potatoes cook for the same amount of time, for example. You may also find that your particular brand or model of pressure cooker cooks faster or even a bit slower. Therefore, feel free to note any cooking time differences in the right-hand column of the table.

Table 4-1	Recommended Pressure Cooker Cooking Times	
Food	**Cooking Time (in Minutes)**	**Your Notes**
Apples, chunks	2	
Artichokes, whole	8 to 10	
Asparagus, whole	1 to 2	
Barley, pearl	15 to 20	
Beans, fresh green or wax, whole or pieces	2 to 3	
Beans, lima, shelled	2 to 3	
Beets, ¼-inch slices	3 to 4	
Beets, whole peeled	12 to 14	
Broccoli, florets or spears	2 to 3	
Brussels sprouts, whole	3 to 4	
Cabbage, red or green, quartered	3 to 4	
Carrots, ¼-inch slices	1 to 2	
Cauliflower, florets	2 to 3	
Chicken, pieces	8 to 10	
Chicken, whole	15 to 20	
Corn on the cob	3 to 4	

(continued)

Table 4-1 *(continued)*

Food	Cooking Time (in Minutes)	Your Notes
Meat (beef, pork, or lamb), roast	40 to 60	
Meat (beef, pork, or lamb),1-inch cubes	15 to 20	
Peas, shelled	1 to 1½	
Potatoes, pieces or sliced	5 to 7	
Potatoes, whole, small or new	5 to 7	
Potatoes, whole, medium	10 to 12	
Rice, brown	15 to 20	
Rice, white	5 to 7	
Spinach, fresh,	2 to 3	
Squash, fall, 1-inch chunks	4 to 6	
Squash, summer, sliced	1 to 2	
Stock	30	
Sweet potatoes, 1½-inch chunks	4 to 5	
Turnips, sliced	2 to 3	

Another way to figure out how long to cook something is by following a similar recipe in this book. Match up your traditional recipe to a pressure cooker one and modify the cooking steps and times accordingly.

Filling the Pressure Cooker

A 6-quart pressure cooker is the ideal size for preparing most recipes that yield 4 to 6 servings. Remember, however, that the pot must never be filled with 6 quarts of anything. In fact, pressure cookers should never be filled more than two-thirds full. The reasons are quite simple. Because a pressure cooker cooks hotter than boiling water, the cooking liquid in the pot seems to expand and increase in volume with all of the bubbling going on. Furthermore, the steam produced by this constant boiling also needs room in which to be contained. If filled more than two-thirds full, the pressure cooker may not perform properly, and you may find cooking liquid coming out the pressure indicator and release valves.

Best Ingredients for Pressure-Cooking

Although you can cook almost anything in a pressure cooker, some foods are better suited than others for this appliance. Foods that normally cook quickly, such as seafood, shellfish, and soft fruits (berries, for example) are better suited for conventional cooking methods. Soups, stocks, stews, and braised and slow-roasted meats made with less expensive cuts of meat, some poultry, steamed and braised vegetables, dried beans and grains, and slow-simmered recipes such as tomato sauce and fruit preserves are ideal candidates for the pressure cooker. The following are some tips for preparing different types of foods.

Meat and poultry

The following are some tips for cooking meat and poultry in the pressure cooker. Because many cuts of meat generally take so long to cook using conventional cooking methods, you'll be surprised and pleased how quickly they cook up in the pressure cooker.

- ✔ Always pat meat and poultry dry before seasoning with salt and freshly ground black pepper.

- ✔ Sear and brown meat in hot oil for the best flavor and texture, unless otherwise indicated in the recipe.

- ✔ Poultry can be prepared with or without the skin.

- ✔ Tougher, less expensive cuts of meat are better suited for the pressure cooker because cooking under pressure breaks the fibers down for fork-tender results.

- ✔ When in doubt, check the cooking temperatures chart for meat in Chapter 8 to make sure that the meat or poultry is adequately cooked.

- ✔ Always let cooked roasts and whole poultry sit for 10 to 15 minutes before carving.

- ✔ Most roasts should be sliced against the grain.

- ✔ For more detailed information on cooking meat and poultry, consult Chapters 7 and 8.

Fruits and vegetables

Fruits and vegetables cook quickly in the pressure cooker, so always use an accurate kitchen timer. Here are some tips for cooking fruits and vegetables in the pressure cooker:

- ✔ Some pressure cooker manufacturers recommend cooking fresh fruit on low pressure, which is a wise thing to do because fruit is soft and cooks quite fast. The only fruits I usually cook in a pressure cooker are apples for applesauce or dried fruits for a compote. These do well on high pressure.

- ✔ Cut thoroughly washed fruits and vegetables into equal-size pieces.

- ✔ When making a stew or pot roast, add vegetables toward the end of the cooking time so that they don't overcook.

- ✔ When cooking only fruits and vegetables, steam them in a steaming basket placed on a trivet in the cooking liquid. This way, they'll retain their flavor and bright color.

- ✔ Always release pressure with a quick-release method (see Chapter 2).

- ✔ For more detailed information on cooking fruits and vegetables, consult Chapters 9 and 10.

Dried beans, legumes, and grains

If I could use my pressure cooker for cooking only two types of food, they would, without a doubt, be beans and grains, which seem to take forever when cooked the conventional way. Here are some tips for cooking dried beans, legumes, and grains in the pressure cooker:

- ✔ Pick over dried beans, legumes, and grains to remove any pebbles, twigs, dirt, or foreign particles. Rinse under cold water.

- ✔ Soak dried beans and legumes, with the exception of lentils and split peas, overnight in room temperature water, or before cooking in boiling water for one hour.

- ✔ Always cook these foods in at least twice as much liquid. For example, for every 1 cup of dried beans, legumes, or grain, cook in 2 cups of water.

- ✔ Never add salt to the cooking liquid when cooking dried beans or legumes because it toughens the skin. Add salt after the food is cooked.

- ✔ You can add a tablespoon of oil to the water to reduce the foaming that beans often cause.

- ✔ For more detailed information on cooking dried beans, legumes, and grains, consult Chapter 6.

Liquids

Never lose sight of the fact that a pressure cooker can't work without liquid. Without liquid, you won't have steam, and without steam, there'll be no pressure. But liquid, as you will see, can be much more than plain old water.

- ✔ All kinds of cooking liquids can be used in the pressure cooker. These may include water, broth or stock, fruit juice, vegetable puree, wine, beer, and so on.

- ✔ With the exception of soups, broth, stock, and sauces, the amount of liquid used in a pressure cooker recipe is usually less than that used in a traditional recipe. Because you're cooking in a sealed pot for a much shorter period of time, less liquid evaporates.

- ✔ When converting a recipe, use approximately one-third to one-half of the liquid called for in the traditional recipe. However, most pressure cookers need at least 1 to 2 cups of liquid in order to build up and maintain pressure. Check the owner's manual for the exact amount needed.

- ✔ Never fill the pressure cooker more than half full with cooking liquid.

Converting My Favorite Recipes for the Pressure Cooker

Although I know you'll enjoy the recipes that I developed especially for this book, I also know that at times you'll want to eat something of your own creation. To show you how to convert your own recipes for use in the pressure cooker, I chose four of my all-time favorite recipes and adapted them. In making my selection, I looked for recipes that, although perhaps not exactly difficult to prepare, had long cooking times or were somewhat labor-intensive, requiring frequent stirring and pot watching. The pressure cooker versions of these original recipes, on the other hand, can save you time and work. After the pressure cooker cover is locked in position and the cooking pressure is reached and stabilized, you're no longer needed in the kitchen until the timer goes off announcing that dinner is ready!

I give you both versions of the recipe, the original version and the pressure cooker adaptation, as well as information on what I did to adapt it. I hope that you, too, will be inspired to experiment and convert some of your favorite traditional recipes for use in the pressure cooker.

Traditional Meat Sauce

This is my mom's recipe for basic meat sauce. She used to make it specifically for preparing pasta dishes such as lasagne and stuffed shells. To save time, she made the sauce a day in advance. If only she had had a pressure cooker!

Preparation time: *10 minutes*

Cooking time: *110 minutes*

Yield: *8 servings*

2 tablespoons olive oil

1 small onion, finely chopped

2 cloves garlic, minced

1 carrot, finely chopped

1 stalk celery, finely chopped

1½ pounds lean ground beef

¼ cup flat-leaf Italian parsley, chopped (see Figure 4-1)

2 cans (28 ounces each) or 7 cups tomato puree

1 teaspoon sugar

4 teaspoons salt

1 teaspoon pepper

1 Heat the olive oil in a 6-quart saucepan over medium-high heat. Add the onion, garlic, carrot, and celery. Cook until the onion is soft. Add the ground beef and cook until no longer pink, breaking up large chunks with a spoon. Add the parsley, tomato puree, sugar, salt, and pepper.

2 Bring the sauce to a boil. Lower the heat. Cover and cook at a simmer for 90 minutes, stirring every 10 minutes.

3 Remove from the heat. Season to taste with salt and pepper. Serve over pasta cooked *al dente* (tender but still firm).

Per serving: *Calories 291 (From Fat 132); Fat 15g (Saturated 5g); Cholesterol 56mg; Sodium 2,001mg; Carbohydrate 22g (Dietary Fiber 5g); Protein 20g.*

MINCING PARSLEY + OTHER FRESH HERBS

1. RINSE AND DRY WELL.

2. CHOP ROUGHLY

3. GATHER AND CHOP SOME MORE! USE A ROCKING MOTION

MOVE KNIFE AROUND

Figure 4-1: Technique for chopping parsley.

✱ NOTE: FOR HERBS LIKE ROSEMARY AND THYME, REMOVE AND CHOP LEAVES. DISCARD THICK STEM.

Pressure Cooker Meat Sauce

I usually like to simmer my meat sauce for at least 90 minutes. But even when time is short and the family's hungry, I still don't have to open a jar of sauce. Instead I turn to my trusty pressure cooker. This was a very easy recipe to adapt. The only thing that needed changing was the cooking time. I was able to shave 60 minutes off my mom's recipe. Everything else stayed the same.

Preparation time: *25 minutes*

Cooking time: *30 minutes under pressure*

Pressure level: *High*

Yield: *8 servings*

2 tablespoons olive oil

1 small onion, finely chopped

2 cloves garlic, minced

1 carrot, finely chopped

1 stalk celery, finely chopped

1½ pounds lean ground beef

¼ cup flat-leaf parsley, chopped (refer back to Figure 4-1)

2 cans (28 ounces each) or 7 cups tomato puree

1 teaspoon sugar

4 teaspoons salt

1 teaspoon pepper

1 Heat the olive oil in a pressure cooker over medium-high heat. Add the onion, garlic, carrot, and celery. Cook until the onion is soft. Add the ground beef and cook until no longer pink, breaking up large chunks with a spoon. Add the parsley, tomato puree, sugar, salt, and pepper.

2 Cover and bring to high pressure over high heat. Lower the heat to stabilize pressure. Cook for 30 minutes.

3 Remove from the heat. Release pressure with a quick-release method. Open and remove the cover.

4 Season to taste. Serve over pasta cooked al dente.

Tip: *If you have a food processor, use it to chop the onions, garlic, carrots, and celery. Begin by placing the onion and garlic in the food processor bowl. Press pulse a couple times until coarsely chopped. Add the carrot and celery (cut into 1-inch pieces) and pulse a couple of times until finely chopped.*

Per serving: *Calories 291 (From Fat 132); Fat 15g (Saturated 5g); Cholesterol 56mg; Sodium 2,001mg; Carbohydrate 22g (Dietary Fiber 5g); Protein 20g.*

◔ Traditional Minestrone Soup

Made with eight different vegetables and fragrant herbs and spices, this Italian classic is the quintessential vegetable soup. Serve with fruit and fresh, crusty bread for a quick and easy complete meal.

Preparation time: *15 minutes*

Cooking time: *50 minutes*

Yield: *6 to 8 servings*

3 tablespoons olive oil

1 medium onion, chopped

3 cloves garlic, minced

1 tablespoon dried Italian seasoning

1 can (14½ ounces) basil-, oregano-, and garlic-flavored diced tomatoes

1 cup diced carrots

1 cup diced celery

1 cup diced zucchini

1 cup peeled and diced potatoes

1 cup bite-sized pieces of string beans

1 tablespoon salt

½ teaspoon pepper

8 cups water

2 cups shredded cabbage

1 can (19 ounces) red kidney beans, drained and rinsed under cold water

1½ cups ditalini (small, tube-shaped pasta), cooked al dente

½ cup freshly grated Parmesan or pecorino Romano cheese

Salt and pepper to taste

1 Heat the olive oil in a 6-quart saucepan over medium-high heat. Add the onion, garlic, and Italian seasoning. Cook until the onion is soft. Add the tomatoes, carrots, celery, zucchini, and potatoes and cook for 5 minutes. Add the string beans, salt, pepper, and water. Stir well.

2 Bring to a boil over high heat. Lower the heat. Cover and cook at a simmer for 45 minutes, stirring every 10 minutes.

3 Add the cabbage and kidney beans. Cover and cook for 10 minutes longer.

4 Add the ditalini and Parmesan cheese. Season with salt and pepper.

Per serving: *Calories 255 (From Fat 69); Fat 8g (Saturated 2g); Cholesterol 5mg; Sodium 1,359mg; Carbohydrate 38g (Dietary Fiber 6g); Protein 11g.*

ᗡ *Pressure Cooker Minestrone Soup*

With my pressure cooker adaptation of minestrone soup, you'll have dinner on the table in half an hour and will never have to resort to canned soups anymore!

Because cabbage takes on a pungent taste and smell when cooked too long, it is added toward the end of the cooking time in the original recipe. I was able to shorten the entire cooking time from 50 to a very short 10 minutes for this version, so you can now add the cabbage along with the other veggies.

Preparation time: 20 minutes

Cooking time: 10 minutes under pressure

Pressure level: High

Yield: 6 to 8 servings

3 tablespoons olive oil

1 medium onion, chopped

3 cloves garlic, minced (see Figure 4-2)

1 tablespoon dried Italian seasoning

1 can (14½ ounces) basil-, oregano-, and garlic-flavored diced tomatoes

1 cup diced carrots

1 cup diced celery

1 cup diced zucchini

1 cup peeled and diced potatoes

1 cup bite-sized pieces of string beans

2 cups shredded cabbage

1 tablespoon salt

½ teaspoon pepper

8 cups water

1 can (19 ounces) red kidney beans, drained and rinsed under cold water

1½ cups ditalini (small, tube-shaped pasta), cooked al dente

½ cup freshly grated Parmesan or pecorino Romano cheese

Salt and pepper to taste

1 Heat the olive oil in the pressure cooker over medium-high heat. Add the onion, garlic, and Italian seasoning. Cook until the onion is soft. Add the tomatoes, carrots, celery, zucchini, and potatoes and cook for 5 minutes. Add the string beans, cabbage, salt, black pepper, and water. Stir well.

2 Cover and bring to high pressure over high heat. Lower the heat to stabilize the pressure. Cook for 10 minutes.

3 Remove from the heat. Release the pressure with a quick-release method. Open and remove the cover.

4 Add the kidney beans, ditalini, and Parmesan cheese. Season with salt and pepper.

Per serving: Calories 255 (From Fat 69); Fat 8g (Saturated 2g); Cholesterol 5mg; Sodium 1,359mg; Carbohydrate 38g (Dietary Fiber 6g); Protein 11g.

Figure 4-2:
Mincing
garlic.

🍅 Traditional Mushroom Risotto

You've probably enjoyed this classic dish at your favorite Italian restaurant, and now you can make it at home. This simple recipe requires a simmering flavorful broth and short-grain Italian rice.

Preparation time: *10 minutes*

Cooking time: *28 minutes*

Yield: *4 servings*

2½ cups chicken or vegetable broth	1 cup Italian Arborio or other short-grain rice
3 tablespoons unsalted butter	⅓ cup grated Parmesan cheese
1 small onion, finely chopped	Pepper to taste
8 ounces white button or crimini mushrooms, sliced (see Figure 4-3)	

1 Bring the broth to a simmer in a small saucepan. Continue simmering.

2 Melt the butter in a 3-quart pot over medium heat. Add the onion and cook until soft. Do not brown. Add the mushrooms and cook for 2 minutes. Add the rice and cook for 1 minute to coat in the butter. Stirring continuously, add about ½ cup of the hot broth. As the rice absorbs the broth, add another ½ cup. Repeat the process, stirring continuously, until there is no more broth and the risotto is cooked al dente.

3 Remove from the heat. Stir in the Parmesan cheese and season with pepper.

Per serving: *Calories 363 (From Fat 124); Fat 14g (Saturated 8g); Cholesterol 33mg; Sodium 781mg; Carbohydrate 48g (Dietary Fiber 2g); Protein 9g.*

How to Trim and Slice Mushrooms

Figure 4-3: Trimming and slicing mushrooms

1. wipe away dirt using a paper towel or a dish towel

2.

Cut off stem

3. slice

⏱ *Pressure Cooker Mushroom Risotto*

If you love risotto but don't have the time to spend 20 minutes standing at the stove stirring a *slowly* simmering saucepan of rice and broth, try this pressure cooker version of the recipe. Risotto made in the pressure cooker is equally as great as the traditional recipe! The rapid bubbling of the broth and rice in the pressure cooker under high pressure replaces my having to stand over a hot stove stirring constantly. Because there is virtually no evaporation, I cut back on the broth by ¼ cup.

Preparation time: *10 minutes*

Cooking time: *7 minutes under pressure*

Pressure level: *High*

Yield: *4 servings*

3 tablespoons unsalted butter

1 small onion, finely chopped

8 ounces white button or crimini mushrooms, sliced

1 cup Italian Arborio or other short-grain rice

2¼ cups chicken or vegetable broth

⅓ cup grated Parmesan cheese

Pepper to taste

1 Melt the butter in a pressure cooker over medium heat. Add the onion and cook until soft. Add the mushrooms and cook for 2 minutes. Add the rice and cook for another 2 minutes. Add the broth and stir to combine.

2 Cover and bring to high pressure. Lower the heat to stabilize pressure and cook for 7 minutes. Release pressure with a quick-release method. Open and remove the cover.

3 Stir in the Parmesan cheese. Season with pepper.

Per serving: *Calories 361 (From Fat 122); Fat 14g (Saturated 8g); Cholesterol 33mg; Sodium 719mg; Carbohydrate 48g (Dietary Fiber 2g); Protein 9g.*

Traditional Sauerbraten

With a delicious balance of sweet and tangy flavors, this German pot roast is an American favorite. Because the meat must marinate three days in the brine before cooking, plan accordingly.

Preparation time: *3 days to marinate meat*

Cooking time: *2 hours, 30 minutes*

Yield: *6 to 8 servings*

4-pound beef chuck or rump roast	*½ cup dry red wine*
2 large carrots, coarsely chopped	*¼ cup firmly packed brown sugar*
2 stalks celery, coarsely chopped	*1 teaspoon ground cloves*
2 large onions, coarsely chopped	*2 teaspoons salt*
1 clove garlic, crushed	*Salt and pepper*
2 bay leaves	*2 tablespoons vegetable oil*
1 cup water	*¾ cup finely crushed gingersnaps*
½ cup red wine vinegar	

1 Place the meat, carrots, celery, onions, garlic, and bay leaves in a large glass or stainless steel bowl. In another bowl, combine the water, vinegar, wine, brown sugar, ground cloves, and 2 teaspoons salt. Pour over the meat. The meat should be submerged in the marinade. If not, transfer to a smaller container. Cover and refrigerate for 3 days.

2 Remove the meat from the marinade. Pat dry with paper towels. Generously salt and pepper.

3 Heat the oil in a Dutch oven over medium-high heat. Brown the meat evenly on all sides.

4 Pour in the reserved marinade and vegetables. Cover and bring to a boil. Lower the heat and simmer until the meat is fork-tender, about 2 hours.

5 Remove the meat to a serving platter and cover with foil. Discard the bay leaves. Add the gingersnaps to the cooking liquid to make a gravy. Stir until well blended. Pour the gravy into a food processor or food mill and process until smooth. Season to taste. Slice the meat across the grain into thick slices and serve with the gravy on the side. Serve with broad egg noodles or Grandma's Mashed Potatoes in Chapter 9.

Per serving: Calories 685 (From Fat 406); Fat 45g (Saturated 19g); Cholesterol 155mg; Sodium 855mg; Carbohydrate 24g (Dietary Fiber 2g); Protein 44g.

Pressure Cooker Sauerbraten

Besides cutting the cooking time in half, this pressure cooker adaptation of my favorite sauerbraten recipe also eliminates the need to first marinate the meat for three days. The rich flavor of the marinade infuses through the roast as it cooks under high pressure.

Preparation time: *20 minutes*

Cooking time: *60 minutes under pressure*

Pressure level: *High*

Yield: *6 to 8 servings*

1 cup water	*2 tablespoons vegetable oil*
½ cup red wine vinegar	*2 large carrots, coarsely chopped*
½ cup dry red wine	*2 stalks celery, coarsely chopped*
¼ cup firmly packed brown sugar	*2 large onions, coarsely chopped*
1 teaspoon ground cloves	*1 clove garlic, crushed*
2 teaspoons salt	*¾ cup finely crushed gingersnaps*
Salt and pepper	*2 bay leaves*
4-pound beef chuck or rump roast	

1 Combine the water, vinegar, wine, brown sugar, cloves, and 2 teaspoons salt. Set aside.

2 Generously salt and pepper the meat.

3 Heat the oil in a pressure cooker over medium-high heat. Brown the meat evenly on all sides.

4 Add the carrots, celery, onions, garlic, crushed gingersnaps, and bay leaves. Pour the mixture from Step 1 over the meat. Stir to combine. Cover and bring to high pressure. Lower the heat to stabilize pressure and cook for 60 minutes.

5 Remove from the heat. Release pressure using a quick-release method. Open and remove the cover.

6 Remove the meat to a serving platter and cover with foil. Discard the bay leaves. To make the gravy, pour the cooking liquid into a food processor or food mill and process until smooth. Season to taste. Slice the meat across the grain into thick slices and serve with the gravy on the side. Serve with broad egg noodles or Grandma's Mashed Potatoes in Chapter 9.

Per serving: Calories 685 (From Fat 406); Fat 45g (Saturated 19g); Cholesterol 155mg; Sodium 855mg; Carbohydrate 24g (Dietary Fiber 2g); Protein 44g.

Part III

Getting Dinner on the Table: Basic and Delicious Recipes for the Pressure Cooker

The 5th Wave   By Rich Tennant

ADAPTATION OF THE PRESSURE COOKER:
THE PRESSURE LOCOMOTIVE
TRAVELED FROM CHEYENNE, WYOMING TO LARAMIE
ON 600 lbs. OF COAL AND 900 HEADS OF BROCCOLI

In this part . . .

I share with you some of my favorite pressure cooker recipes for dinner in Chapters 5 through 8. These run the gamut from soups and pilafs, to an amazing variety of bean dishes, to succulent roasts and stews. All are quick and easy to prepare and delicious to eat!

Chapter 5

Spoon Foods: Soups and Great Grain Dishes

In This Chapter

▶ Coaxing out the flavor in soups

▶ Cooking grains

. . . .

1 always find it reassuring to eat almost anything from an oversized bowl with a big spoon. I guess I'm not alone, because many restaurants are serving diners all kinds of comfort foods in soup bowls nearly the size of serving pieces.

Soupy-type foods are among my favorites. They're warm and nourishing. Although some also contain meat or poultry, they almost always have lots of good vegetables in a flavorful broth or sauce. Some are smooth in consistency, and others are so chunky that you may want to eat them with a fork. Whatever your preference, these are dishes that taste good and make you feel warm and cozy all over.

Recipes in This Chapter

▶ Chicken Stock

▶ Beef Stock

▶ Chunky Chicken Noodle Soup

▶ Corn Chowder

▶ French Onion Soup

▶ Warm Louisiana Yam Soup with Snipped Chives

▶ Potato and Leek Potage

▶ Creamy Cauliflower Soup

▶ Split Pea Soup

↻ Citrusy Grain Salad

↻ Basic Quinoa Recipe

↻ Basic Pearl Barley Recipe

▶ Beef Barley Mushroom Soup

▶ Arroz con Pollo

↻ Spanish Rice

▶ Yellow Split Pea and Basmati Pilaf

▶ Bulgur Pilaf

Soup under Pressure

Good soup normally simmers to allow the cooking liquid to slowly coax out all the different flavors from the ingredients as they blend together to create a delicious, flavorful broth. The pressure cooker is unique in that it allows this flavor mingling but at a much higher temperature in a fraction of the time.

Making stock

The first place to start in making great soup is with full-flavored cooking liquid or stock. To make stock, you cook lots of vegetables, alone or with poultry, meat, or seafood, in less water than you normally would use in making soup. Traditional, slow simmered stock takes up to 2 to 3 hours to make; pressure cooker stock takes about one-third of the time: 30 minutes of cooking under pressure and about another 30 minutes for the pressure to drop on its own.

Regardless of the method you use, once the stock is done, you need to remove the solid ingredients with a slotted spoon and filter the remaining liquid through a fine mesh strainer. Because most of the flavor from the solids has been extracted, they're for the most part now flavorless and should be discarded, except for perhaps meaty chicken pieces that you can remove from the bone and reserve for adding to soup or making chicken salad.

Using and storing stock

As far as using the rich, flavorful stock goes, it makes a great base for soups, or you can boil some of it down to concentrate the flavor even more to make sauces or gravies. After cutting the fat (see Figure 5-1), I freeze any leftover stock to have on hand. Sometimes I even freeze reduced stock in ice cube trays. Once frozen, I store the concentrated stock cubes in small plastic bags to use when a recipe calls for a small amount of stock or broth.

Freezer space is always an issue for me. I never seem to have enough of it, and plastic containers take up a lot of valuable space. I like to freeze liquids such as sauces, soups, and stocks in 1-quart or 1-gallon resealable plastic freezer bags. Always write on the outside what's in the bag and the date it was frozen, so you know exactly what's in it and how long it's been in there. After filling the bag, seal it, carefully squeezing out as much air as possible. Wipe off any spilled food and lay the bag flat in the freezer, stacking the bags on top of each other.

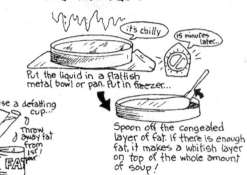

Figure 5-1:
Defatting
your broth.

Salt in soups, broths, and stocks

Salt is added to food to enhance flavor. Stocks, broths, and soups will have little taste if not salted adequately, even if they are made with many flavorful ingredients such as poultry, meat, and vegetables. Unless you're on a sodium-restricted diet, don't be alarmed by the amount of salt you need to use to get the desired flavor. Start off with a couple of teaspoons and gradually add more, little by little, until you achieve the desired flavor. For those of you on a sodium-restricted or reduced-sodium diet, try replacing the salt with other flavorful ingredients such as celery seed and garlic or onion powder.

Chicken Stock

Whenever I buy a whole chicken to cut up, I always put aside the neck, wings, and back. I freeze these in a large plastic bag. When I've accumulated enough pieces, I take them out and make a big pot of stock; if I'm in a rush and come up short, I add some legs or thighs from the supermarket.

Preparation time: *10 minutes*

Cooking time: *30 minutes under pressure*

Pressure level: *High*

Yield: *Approximately 2 quarts*

3 to 4 pounds of chicken pieces (necks, wings, backs, legs, and thighs), with skin

1 large onion, peeled and quartered

3 carrots, cut into 1-inch pieces

3 stalks celery, cut into 1-inch pieces

1 parsnip, cut into 1-inch pieces

1 large tomato, quartered

3 cloves garlic

2 sprigs parsley

½ teaspoon whole black peppercorns

8 cups (2 quarts) water

Salt to taste

1 Rinse the chicken pieces under cold water. Place the chicken, onion, carrots, celery, parsnip, tomato, garlic, parsley, peppercorns, and water in a pressure cooker.

2 Cover and bring to high pressure over high heat. Lower the heat to stabilize the pressure. Cook for 30 minutes.

3 Remove from the heat. Let the pressure drop using the natural-release method.

4 Unlock and remove the cover. Let the stock cool to room temperature.

5 Remove the chicken and vegetables. Remove the chicken from the bone; dice and save for another use. Discard all of the vegetables with a slotted spoon. Pour the stock through a fine strainer into a large storage container. Season with salt.

6 Refrigerate overnight. Remove and discard any congealed fat (see Figure 5-1).

Vary It! *Next time you roast a turkey, save the carcass after carving to make great stock. Simply rinse under water and place in the pressure cooker pot instead of the chicken pieces. If the carcass is too big, simply, compact it by pressing down with the heel of your hand on a hard, clean work surface.*

Vary It! *For quick and easy vegetable stock, simply eliminate the chicken all together and double up on the veggies.*

Per serving: *Calories 29 (From Fat 16); Fat 2g (Saturated 1g); Cholesterol 1mg; Sodium 295mg; Carbohydrate 3g (Dietary Fiber 0g); Protein 1g.*

Beef Stock

There is more than one way to make beef stock, depending on your mood and the time available. I will either be lazy and throw the bones into the pot to make a very acceptable, good-flavored beef stock, or if I have time, I salt and pepper the bones and roast them until golden brown in a 400-degree oven for about 45 minutes to an hour. After roasting the bones, I then prepare the stock as detailed here, blotting the bones with paper towels to remove any melted fat. The ensuing stock is deeper in flavor and darker in color than the stock that you get by the quicker method.

Preparation time: *10 minutes*

Cooking time: *30 minutes, under pressure*

Pressure level: *High*

Yield: *Approximately 2 quarts*

3 pounds meaty beef bones	*3 sprigs parsley*
1 large onion, peeled and quartered	*1 bay leaf*
3 carrots, cut into 1-inch pieces	*½ teaspoon whole black peppercorns*
3 stalks celery, cut into 1-inch pieces	*8 cups (2 quarts) water*
2 large tomatoes, quartered	*Salt to taste*
3 cloves garlic	

1 Rinse the bones under cold water. Place the bones, onion, carrots, celery, tomatoes, garlic, parsley, bay leaf, peppercorns, and water in a pressure cooker.

2 Cover and bring to high pressure over high heat. Lower the heat to stabilize the pressure. Cook for 30 minutes.

3 Remove from the heat. Let the pressure drop using the natural-release method.

4 Unlock and remove the cover. Let the stock cool to room temperature.

5 Remove and discard the bones and all of the vegetables with a slotted spoon. Pour through a fine strainer into a large storage container. Season with salt.

6 Refrigerate overnight. Remove and discard any congealed fat.

Per serving: *Calories 29 (From Fat 9); Fat 1g (Saturated 0g); Cholesterol 1mg; Sodium 39mg; Carbohydrate 5g (Dietary Fiber 0g); Protein 1g.*

Chunky Chicken Noodle Soup

Touted as a cure for the common cold, chicken soup nourishes the belly as well as the soul. Although this soup is usually slowly simmered to extract the natural goodness from the ingredients, you can now enjoy this restorative elixir in a fraction of the time by making it in a pressure cooker.

Preparation time: *10 minutes*

Cooking time: *19 minutes under pressure*

Pressure setting: *High*

Yield: *4 to 6 servings*

2 split chicken breasts with bone and skin, about 1½ pounds

8 cups (2 quarts) water

1 tablespoon salt

2 large leeks (or 1 large onion) washed well to remove dirt and grit, white and light green parts only, thinly sliced

3 carrots, peeled and cut into ¼-inch rounds

3 stalks celery, cut into ¼-inch slices

Salt and pepper to taste

2 cups broad egg noodles, cooked al dente

1 tablespoon chopped fresh parsley or snipped dill

1 Rinse the chicken under water. Place in a pressure cooker with the water and 1 tablespoon salt.

2 Cover and bring to high pressure over high heat. Lower the heat to stabilize the pressure. Cook for 15 minutes.

3 Remove from the heat. Let the pressure drop using a quick-release method.

4 Unlock and remove the cover.

5 Remove the chicken with a slotted spoon. Skin and debone the chicken. Cut into bite-sized chunks and set aside.

6 Pour the broth through a fine strainer into a 3-quart container. Rinse out the pressure cooker and pour the broth back into it. Add the leeks, carrots, and celery.

7 Cover and bring to high pressure over high heat. Lower the heat to stabilize the pressure. Cook for 4 minutes.

8 Remove from the heat. Let the pressure drop using a quick-release method.

9 Unlock and remove the cover. Season with salt and pepper.

10 Add the cooked chicken, noodles, and parsley.

Per serving: Calories 125 (From Fat 16); Fat 2g (Saturated 0g); Cholesterol 43mg; Sodium 937mg; Carbohydrate 11g (Dietary Fiber 2g); Protein 15g.

☙ *Corn Chowder*

Corn chowder, full of pieces of colorful vegetables and thicker than chicken soup, is one of my favorite soups. I find that if I cook the noodles directly in the soup, they release some starch, which thickens the broth and adds more body. For a more complete, one-bowl dinner, I sometimes add some diced chicken that I saved when I made the stock.

Preparation time: *10 minutes*

Cooking time: *8 minutes under pressure*

Pressure setting: *High*

Yield: *4 to 6 servings*

2 tablespoons vegetable oil

1 small onion, chopped (see Figure 5-2)

1 red bell pepper, cored, seeded, and diced

2 carrots, peeled and cut into ¼-inch rounds

2 stalks celery, cut into ¼-inch slices

1 large all-purpose potato, peeled and diced

2 cups frozen corn kernels

1 cup frozen green peas

6 cups chicken or vegetable stock or broth

Salt and pepper to taste

2 cups broad egg noodles

1 tablespoon chopped fresh parsley or snipped dill

2 cups cooked diced chicken (optional)

1 Heat the vegetable oil in a pressure cooker over medium-high heat. Add the onion and red pepper. Cook until the onion is soft. Add the carrots, celery, potato, corn, and peas. Cook for 2 minutes. Add the stock.

2 Cover and bring to high pressure over high heat. Lower the heat to stabilize the pressure. Cook for 8 minutes.

3 Remove from the heat. Let the pressure drop using a quick-release method.

4 Unlock and remove the cover.

5 Season with salt and pepper. Bring the chowder to a boil. Add the noodles and cook until al dente. Stir in the parsley and, if desired, the chicken. Serve immediately.

Per serving: *Calories 165 (From Fat 50); Fat 6g (Saturated 1g); Cholesterol 9mg; Sodium 341mg; Carbohydrate 26g (Dietary Fiber 4g); Protein 5g.*

French Onion Soup

Some onion soups are short on onions and flavor, but not this one! Excluding the bread and cheese, there are only six basic ingredients in this soup, but what ingredients they are: flavorful olive oil, sweet onions, pungent garlic (both onions and garlic are members of the allium family; see Figure 5-3), enticing thyme, mellow dry sherry, and rich beef broth stock! When combined, they make for the best onion soup, especially when topped with crisp bread croutons and melted cheese.

Preparation time: *15 minutes*

Cooking time: *6 minutes under pressure*

Pressure setting: *High*

Yield: *4 to 6 servings*

1½ cups of ¾-inch square French bread cubes	1 tablespoon dried thyme
4 tablespoons olive oil	⅔ cup dry sherry or white vermouth
6 cups thinly sliced Spanish or Vidalia onions	4 cups beef stock or broth
4 cloves garlic, sliced thin	Salt and pepper to taste
	1 cup grated Gruyère or Swiss cheese

1 Preheat the oven to 350°. Toss the bread cubes in a large bowl with 2 tablespoons of the olive oil. Place on a baking sheet and toast in a 350° oven for 15 minutes, or until crisp, shaking periodically. Set aside to cool.

2 Heat the remaining 2 tablespoons olive oil in the pressure cooker over medium-high heat. Add the onions and garlic. Cook for 5 minutes. Add the thyme, dry sherry, and 2 cups of the stock.

3 Cover and bring to high pressure over high heat. Lower the heat to stabilize the pressure. Cook for 6 minutes.

4 Remove from the heat. Let the pressure drop using a quick-release method.

5 Unlock and remove the cover.

6 Preheat the broiler. Add the remaining 2 cups of stock and bring to a simmer. Season with salt and pepper.

7 Ladle the soup into heatproof bowls. Float some bread cubes on top and sprinkle with the Gruyère cheese. Place the soup bowls on a baking pan and set under the broiler until the cheese melts and is bubbly, about 1 to 3 minutes, depending on your broiler.

Per serving: Calories 246 (From Fat 145); Fat 16g (Saturated 5g); Cholesterol 21mg; Sodium 226mg; Carbohydrate 18g (Dietary Fiber 4g); Protein 8g.

HOW TO CHOP AN ONION

Figure 5-2: Chopping an onion.

1. CUT OFF STEM. CUT IN HALF THROUGH THE ROOT. PEEL OFF & SKIN

2. MAKE PARALLEL LENGTHWISE CUTS. DO NOT CUT THROUGH ROOT END!

3. CUT HORIZONTAL SLICES FROM TOP TO BOTTOM. NOT ALL THE WAY THROUGH.

4. NOW, CUT CROSSWISE!

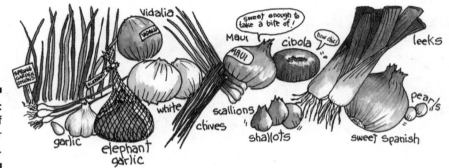

Figure 5-3: Members of the allium or onion family.

spring garden onions · Vidalia · white · garlic · elephant garlic · scallions · chives · Maui · cibola · shallots · sweet enough to take a bite of! · how chic! · leeks · pearls · sweet Spanish

🍅 *Warm Louisiana Yam Soup with Snipped Chives*

I came up with this recipe for culinary appearances I was making in New Orleans. It was late spring, and I wanted to focus on locally grown ingredients, in this case bright orange Louisiana yams. This is a great soup to make and serve year-round. Either serve it warm after adding the milk or simmer longer and serve hot.

Preparation time: *15 minutes*

Cooking time: *10 minutes under pressure*

Pressure setting: *High*

Yield: *4 to 6 servings*

2 tablespoons olive oil

2 pounds yams or sweet potatoes, peeled and cut into 1-inch cubes

1 large onion, chopped

2 cloves garlic, crushed

1½-inch slice fresh gingerroot, peeled and thinly sliced

4 cups (1 quart) vegetable or chicken stock or broth

2 cups milk

Salt to taste

2 tablespoons snipped fresh chives

1 Heat the olive oil in a pressure cooker over medium-high heat. Add the yams, onion, garlic, and gingerroot. Cook for 5 minutes. Add the stock.

2 Cover and bring to high pressure over high heat. Lower the heat to stabilize the pressure. Cook for 10 minutes.

3 Remove from the heat. Let the pressure drop using a quick-release method.

4 Unlock and remove the cover. The yams should be very soft. If they're still hard, return to Step 2 and cook for an additional 2 to 3 minutes, or until tender.

5 Purée the soup with a hand blender in the pressure cooker (or in batches in a blender, then pour back into the pressure cooker), until smooth. Whisk in the milk and warm over low heat. Season with salt. Serve with snipped chives.

Per serving: Calories 415 (From Fat 113); Fat 13g (Saturated 4g); Cholesterol 17mg; Sodium 1,091mg; Carbohydrate 69g (Dietary Fiber 5g); Protein 10g.

The hand blender: My best kitchen buddy (after the pressure cooker, that is)

Did you know that you can purée hot food directly in the pressure cooker (or any pot or bowl, for that matter) if you have a hand blender also known as an immersion blender? Popular overseas for years, this nifty, small electric appliance, approximately 16 to 18 inches long, has been available in the United States for a few years now and makes puréeing hot soups and sauces a breeze. You simply hold the hand blender vertically, inserting the blade part into the food you wish to purée. Push and hold down on the on/off button. With the blade always in the food, you'll purée away as the food is pulled in through the bottom and side cutouts or openings. Naturally, the food must be cooked until very soft and in a liquid base. Never lift the hand blender up and out of the hot food while operating, because you'll get splattered, and possibly burned!

Hand blenders are also great for making malteds and smoothies. Many come with a mini-chopper attachment and, in some cases, even a whisk.

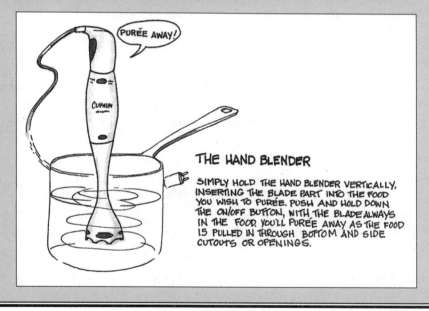

THE HAND BLENDER

SIMPLY HOLD THE HAND BLENDER VERTICALLY, INSERTING THE BLADE PART INTO THE FOOD YOU WISH TO PURÉE. PUSH AND HOLD DOWN THE ON/OFF BUTTON. WITH THE BLADE ALWAYS IN THE FOOD, YOU'LL PURÉE AWAY AS THE FOOD IS PULLED IN THROUGH BOTTOM AND SIDE CUTOUTS OR OPENINGS.

🍅 *Potato and Leek Potage*

Potato and leek potage is a classic French soup. Native to the Mediterranean countries, leeks, which look like long, fat green onions or scallions, are very popular in Europe, where they're sometimes called the poor man's asparagus. Although related to both the onion and the garlic, leeks tend to have a more subtle flavor, which is released as they slowly cook over low heat, as in this delicious, country-style soup.

Preparation time: *15 minutes*

Cooking time: *10 minutes under pressure*

Pressure setting: *High*

Yield: *4 to 6 servings*

2 tablespoons butter

4 large leeks, washed well to remove dirt and grit, white and light green parts only (see Figure 5-4), thinly sliced

5 medium (about 2 pounds) all-purpose potatoes, peeled and thinly sliced

6 cups (1½ quarts) chicken or vegetable stock or broth

1 cup milk

Salt and pepper to taste

1 Heat the butter in a pressure cooker over medium heat. Add the leeks and cook until soft; don't let them brown. Add the potaotes and stock.

2 Cover and bring to high pressure over high heat. Lower the heat to stabilize the pressure. Cook for 10 minutes.

3 Remove from the heat. Let the pressure drop using a quick-release method.

4 Unlock and remove the cover. Potatoes should be very soft. If they're still hard, return to Step 2 and cook them for an additional 2 to 3 minutes, or until tender.

5 Purée the soup with a hand blender or in batches in a blender, until smooth. Pour back into the pressure cooker. Whisk in the milk and warm over low heat. Season with salt and pepper.

Per serving: Calories 253 (From Fat 66); Fat 7g (Saturated 4g); Cholesterol 17mg; Sodium 436mg; Carbohydrate 43g (Dietary Fiber 5g); Protein 5g.

Figure 5-4:
Cleaning a leek.

Creamy Cauliflower Soup

I've been making this soup for as long as I can remember. It has to be one of my easiest and fastest recipes, enjoyed by even those who aren't big fans of cauliflower. The caraway seeds add great flavor. You can easily grind them in a pepper or spice mill.

Preparation time: *15 minutes*

Cooking time: *10 minutes under pressure*

Pressure setting: *High*

Yield: *4 to 6 servings*

2 tablespoons olive oil

1 large onion, chopped

1 large head cauliflower, trimmed and broken into small florets

6 cups (1½ quarts) chicken or vegetable stock or broth

Salt and pepper to taste

1 teaspoon caraway seeds, finely ground

1 Heat the olive oil in a pressure cooker over medium-high heat. Add the onion and cook until soft. Add the cauliflower and stock.

2 Cover and bring to high pressure over high heat. Lower the heat to stabilize the pressure. Cook for 10 minutes.

3 Remove from the heat. Let the pressure drop using a quick-release method.

4 Unlock and remove the cover. The cauliflower should be very soft. If it's still hard, return to Step 2 and cook it for an additional 2 to 3 minutes, or until tender.

5 Purée the soup with a hand blender or in batches in a blender, until smooth. Pour back into the pressure cooker. Season with salt and pepper. Stir in the caraway seeds.

Per serving: Calories 116(From Fat 57); Fat 6g (Saturated 1g); Cholesterol 1mg; Sodium 436mg; Carbohydrate 13g (Dietary Fiber 4g); Protein 4g.

☺ Split Pea Soup

We always have split pea soup during Christmas week, after we finish picking off the last morsel of meat from the Christmas ham, until only the bone remains. When the urge for split pea soup hits at other times of the year, I pick up a small ham steak, cut it into cubes, and add them instead.

Preparation time: *15 minutes*

Cooking time: *10 minutes under pressure*

Pressure setting: *High*

Yield: *4 to 6 servings*

2 cups (1 pound) dried green or yellow split peas, picked over	1 ham bone, or 1 small ham steak, trimmed of all fat and diced
2 tablespoons olive oil	2 teaspoons dry marjoram
1 large onion, chopped	1 teaspoon salt
2 cloves garlic, minced	⅛ teaspoon pepper
1 large potato, peeled and diced	8 cups water
2 carrots, peeled and thinly sliced	Salt and pepper to taste
1 stalk celery, thinly sliced	

1 Rinse the dried peas in a colander under cold water. Heat the olive oil in a pressure cooker over medium heat. Add the onion and garlic. Cook until the onion is soft. Add the potato, carrots, celery, ham bone, marjoram, salt, and pepper. Cook for 2 minutes. Add the split peas and water. Stir well.

2 Cover and bring to high pressure over high heat. Lower the heat to stabilize the pressure. Cook for 10 minutes.

3 Remove from the heat. Let the pressure drop using a quick release method.

4 Unlock and remove the cover.

5 Season with salt and pepper. Stir well.

Per serving: Calories 356 (From Fat 98); Fat 11g (Saturated 3g); Cholesterol 26mg; Sodium 436mg; Carbohydrate 45g (Dietary Fiber 15g); Protein 22g.

The Goodness of Grain

According to the nutrition gurus, everyone should eat 6 to 11 servings of grain each day, which is not always an easy task. Maybe you don't have any new or exciting recipes using grains, or more likely than not, you don't have the time it takes to cook wheat berries, barley, or other grains until they're tender. Well, now that you know you can cook them in no time at all in your pressure cooker, you can come closer to meeting your daily requirement! See Figure 5-5 for different types of grains you can cook.

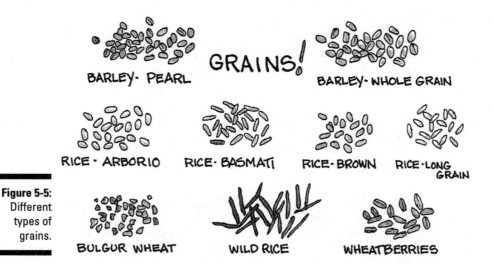

GRAINS!

BARLEY- PEARL   BARLEY- WHOLE GRAIN

RICE - ARBORIO   RICE- BASMATI   RICE- BROWN   RICE - LONG GRAIN

BULGUR WHEAT   WILD RICE   WHEATBERRIES

Figure 5-5:
Different types of grains.

Consider grains as you would dried beans. Although grains don't need to be presoaked, they should be picked over and rinsed in a colander under cold water before cooking. Cook them in ample water because they'll absorb a considerable amount of liquid as they hydrate during cooking. A good general rule is to use 3 to 4 cups of water for each cup of grain, and 2 cups of water for each cup of rice. A cup of uncooked grain becomes 2½ to 3 cups after cooking (see Table 5-1). Cooking times vary depending on the variety of the grain, as well as how old it is.

Table 5-1:	Grain Cooked Yields	
The following chart provides the approximate yield of dried grains after cooking.		
Uncooked Food	*Cooked*	*Water, Plus 1 Tablespoon Oil*
(1 Cup)	*(Cups)*	*(Cups)*
Barley, pearl	3½	4½
Barley, whole (unhulled)	3½	4½
Bulgur wheat, whole grain	3½	4½
Quinoa	3	2½
Rice, arborio	3	2
Rice, basmati	3	1¾
Rice, brown	2¼	1¾
Rice, long grain	3	1¾
Rice, wild	2¼	3
Whole wheatberries	2	4½

The cooking times for grains given in Table 5-2 are, at best, approximations and should be used only as general guidelines. You may also find that your particular brand or model of pressure cooker cooks faster or even a bit slower. Therefore, feel free to note any cooking time differences in the right-hand column of the chart. The addition of oil cuts back on foaming as the grain cooks.

Table 5-2:	Recommended Pressure Cooker Cooking Times for Grains	

The following cooking times begin when the pressure cooker reaches high pressure. Always start with the shortest cooking time; you can always continue cooking under pressure for an additional couple of minutes until the desired texture is reached.

Food	Cooking Time (in Minutes)	Your Notes
Barley, pearl	15 to 20	
Barley, whole (unhulled)	50 to 55	
Bulgur wheat, whole grain	10 to 12	
Quinoa	7	
Rice, arborio	7 to 8	
Rice, basmati	5 to 7	
Rice, brown	15 to 20	
Rice, long-grain	5 to 7	
Rice, wild	22 to 25	
Wheatberries	12 to 15	

☙ *Citrusy Grain Salad*

Although significantly increasing your fiber intake isn't always easy, this tasty salad is one way to get more fiber in your diet. Made with barley and quinoa, an ancient grain first enjoyed by the Andean Incas and readily available at most supermarkets and health food stores, the grains are first cooked separately in the pressure cooker and then tossed with a citrus vinaigrette and dried cranberries to make a show-stopper of a salad.

Preparation time: *10 minutes*

Yield: *4 to 6 servings*

4 cups cooked quinoa, cooled to room temperature (for pressure-cooked quinoa, see Basic Quinoa Recipe that follows)

3½ cups cooked pearl barley, cooled to room temperature (for pressure-cooked barley, see Basic Barley Recipe that follows)

Grated zest of 1 lemon

Grated zest of 1 orange

2 carrots, coarsely grated

2 stalks celery, diced small

4 scallions or green onions, thinly sliced

⅓ cup coarsely chopped flat-leaf Italian parsley

3 tablespoons coarsely chopped mint leaves

⅓ cup dried cranberries

3 tablespoons freshly squeezed lemon juice

⅓ cup extra-virgin olive oil

2 teaspoons Dijon mustard

Salt and pepper to taste

1 Combine the cooked quinoa and barley, lemon and orange zest, carrots, celery, scallions, parsley, mint, and dried cranberries in a large mixing bowl. Toss well.

2 Whisk together the lemon juice, olive oil, and Dijon mustard. Season with salt and black pepper. Pour over the salad and toss. Refrigerate for 1 hour before serving.

Per serving: *Calories 405 (From Fat 132); Fat 15g (Saturated 2g); Cholesterol 0mg; Sodium 184mg; Carbohydrate 63g (Dietary Fiber 8g); Protein 8g.*

↻ *Basic Quinoa Recipe*

Preparation time: *2 minutes*

Cooking time: *7 minutes under pressure*

Pressure setting: *High*

Yield: *approximately 4 cups*

1½ cups quinoa, rinsed and drained   1 tablespoon vegetable oil

3 cups water

1 Combine quinoa, water, and oil in the pressure cooker pot.

2 Cover and bring to high pressure over high heat. Lower the heat to stabilize the pressure. Cook for 7 minutes.

3 Remove from the heat. Let pressure drop using a quick release method.

4 Unlock and remove the cover. The quinoa should be slightly chewy. If hard, return to Step 2 and cook for an additional 1 to 3 minutes, or until tender.

5 Drain the quinoa in a colander or strainer.

Per serving: *Calories 134 (From Fat 32); Fat 4g (Saturated 0g); Cholesterol 0mg; Sodium 7mg; Carbohydrate 22g (Dietary Fiber 2g); Protein 4g.*

☕ *Basic Pearl Barley Recipe*

Preparation time: *2 minutes*

Cooking time: *15 minutes under pressure*

Pressure setting: *High*

Yield: *approximately 4 cups*

1 cup pearl barley, rinsed and drained

4½ cups water

1 tablespoon vegetable oil

1 Combine pearl barley, water, and oil in the pressure cooker pot.

2 Cover and bring to high pressure over high heat. Lower the heat to stabilize the pressure. Cook for 15 minutes.

3 Remove from the heat. Let pressure drop using a quick release method.

4 Unlock and remove the cover. The barley should be slightly chewy. If hard, return to Step 2 and cook for an additional 1 to 3 minutes, or until tender.

5 Drain the barley in a colander or strainer.

Per serving: Calories 103 (From Fat 18); Fat 2g (Saturated 0g); Cholesterol 0mg; Sodium 2mg; Carbohydrate 19g (Dietary Fiber 4g); Protein 2g.

Beef Barley Mushroom Soup

This is definitely a rib-sticking, good-for-you kind of soup. It's chock-full of tender chunks of beef and mushrooms mixed with sliced carrots and celery. The addition of tiny ovals of chewy, pearl barley adds a comforting, old-fashioned twist. Pearl barley is readily available at most supermarkets, usually near the rice.

Preparation time: *15 minutes*

Cooking time: *20 minutes under pressure*

Pressure setting: *High*

Yield: *4 to 6 servings*

2 tablespoons vegetable oil

1 large onion, chopped

½ pound very lean beef stew meat, cut into ½-inch cubes

3 carrots, peeled and thinly sliced

3 stalks celery, thinly sliced

¼ pound white button mushrooms, stems trimmed, quartered

¼ pound shiitake mushrooms, stems trimmed, quartered

1 cup pearl barley, rinsed in a colander under cold water

1 bay leaf

1 teaspoon salt

¼ teaspoon black pepper

6 cups beef or chicken stock or broth

2 cups water

1 tablespoon minced flat leaf, Italian parsley

Salt and pepper to taste

1 Heat vegetable oil in the pressure cooker over medium-high heat. Add the onion and cook until soft. Add the meat, carrots, celery, mushrooms, barley, bay leaf, salt, pepper, and stock and water.

2 Cover and bring to high pressure over high heat. Lower the heat to stabilize the pressure. Cook for 20 minutes.

3 Remove from the heat. Let the pressure drop using a quick-release method.

4 Unlock and remove the cover. Season with salt and pepper. Add the parsley before serving.

Per serving: *Calories 274 (From Fat 74); Fat 8g (Saturated 2g); Cholesterol 24mg; Sodium 474mg; Carbohydrate 39g (Dietary Fiber 8g); Protein 13g.*

Arroz con Pollo

Arroz con pollo, or — as we know it in English — chicken and rice, is a Spanish classic enjoyed with many variations in most Spanish-speaking countries. My version, which I share with you here, is most true to its Iberian origins.

Although this dish is traditionally made in a shallow, steel paella pan, many, if not most, Spanish housewives prefer to use their convenient and quick pressure cooker when making this dish, commonly referred as simply *arroz.*

Preparation time: *15 minutes*

Cooking time: *7 minutes under pressure*

Pressure setting: *High*

Yield: *4 to 6 servings*

Salt and pepper

One 3-pound chicken, skin removed, cut into eighths

3 tablespoons olive oil

1 chorizo sausage, thinly sliced (optional)

½ cup white wine

1 small onion, chopped

2 cloves garlic, peeled and minced

1 red bell pepper, cored, seeded, and diced

1 large ripe tomato, peeled, or 2 canned plum tomatoes, seeded and coarsely chopped

1 cup uncooked long-grain white rice

½ cup frozen peas

3 cups chicken stock or broth

1 teaspoon salt

1 Generously salt and pepper the chicken pieces.

2 Heat 2 tablespoons of the olive oil in a pressure cooker over medium-high heat. Brown the chicken in batches. Set aside on a large plate. Add the chorizo, if desired, and cook for 1 minute. Return the browned chicken to the pressure cooker. Add the wine and cook for 2 minutes. Remove to a plate with any juices and set aside.

3 Heat the remaining 1 tablespoon olive oil in the pressure cooker. Add the onion, garlic, red bell pepper, and tomato. Cook until the onion is soft. Add the rice and cook for 1 minute. Add the peas, stock, salt, chicken, and chorizo, with any accumulated juices. Stir well.

4 Cover and bring to high pressure over high heat. Lower the heat to stabilize the pressure. Cook for 7 minutes.

5 Remove from the heat. Let the pressure drop using a quick-release method.

6 Unlock and remove the cover.

7 Fluff the rice and serve.

Per serving: *Calories 390 (From Fat 147); Fat 16g (Saturated 3g); Cholesterol 61mg; Sodium 639mg; Carbohydrate 33g (Dietary Fiber 2g); Protein 26g.*

☺ Spanish Rice

Never go to Spain and order Spanish rice; they'll have no idea what you're asking for! Spanish rice is most definitely an American creation from the early 1900s. The following recipe cooks the rice directly in a savory tomato sauce.

Preparation time: *15 minutes*

Cooking time: *7 minutes under pressure*

Pressure setting: *High*

Yield: *4 to 6 servings*

2 tablespoons olive oil	3 cans (8 ounces each) tomato sauce
1 large onion, chopped	2 cups water
2 cloves garlic, minced	2 teaspoons salt
1 green bell pepper, cored, seeded, and diced	1/8 teaspoon black pepper
2 cups uncooked long-grain white rice	

1 Heat the olive oil in a pressure cooker over medium-high heat. Add the onion, garlic, and green bell pepper. Cook until the onion is soft. Add the rice and cook for 1 minute. Add the tomato sauce, water, salt, and black pepper.

2 Cover and bring to high pressure over high heat. Lower the heat to stabilize the pressure. Cook for 7 minutes.

3 Remove from the heat. Let the pressure drop using a quick-release method.

4 Unlock and remove the cover.

Per serving: *Calories 340 (From Fat 48); Fat 5g (Saturated 1g); Cholesterol 0mg; Sodium 1,465mg; Carbohydrate 66g (Dietary Fiber 3g); Protein 7g.*

Yellow Split Pea and Basmati Pilaf

With Indian food gaining in popularity nationwide, I have begun to incorporate it into my cooking repertoire when doing cooking presentations. This pilaf recipe combines two very popular Indian grains: basmati rice, a very fragrant, nutty-flavored rice from the foothills of the Himalayas, and yellow *dal,* or split peas, both of which are readily available at most supermarkets.

I like to serve this pilaf with the Indian Butter Chicken in Chapter 8 or the Moroccan Chicken in Chapter 7.

Preparation time: *15 minutes*

Cooking time: *8 minutes under pressure*

Pressure setting: *High*

Yield: *4 to 6 servings*

1 cup basmati rice	2 cups chicken stock or broth
½ cup yellow split peas	¼ cup water
2 tablespoons vegetable oil	¾ teaspoon salt
1 large onion, chopped	⅛ teaspoon pepper
½ teaspoon grated fresh gingerroot	2 tablespoons minced cilantro
1 teaspoon cumin seeds	½ cup chopped dry-roasted cashews

1 Rinse the rice and split peas under cold water. Place in a bowl and cover with cold water. Soak for 10 minutes.

2 Heat the vegetable oil in a pressure cooker over medium-high heat. Add the onion, gingerroot, and cumin seeds. Cook until the onion is soft.

3 Drain the rice mixture, rinse, and add to the pressure cooker with the stock, water, salt, and pepper. Stir well.

4 Cover and bring to high pressure over high heat. Lower the heat to stabilize the pressure. Cook for 8 minutes.

5 Remove from the heat. Let the pressure drop using a quick-release method.

6 Unlock and remove the cover.

7 Add the cilantro and fluff the rice. Spoon into a serving dish and sprinkle with the cashews.

Per serving: Calories 318 (From Fat 100); Fat 11g (Saturated 2g); Cholesterol 6mg; Sodium 396mg; Carbohydrate 45g (Dietary Fiber 2g); Protein 11g.

Bulgur Pilaf

Most Americans are familiar with bulgur wheat only from making *tabbouleh,* a Middle Eastern salad. An Eastern European and Middle Eastern staple, bulgur is nothing more than whole wheat that has been washed, steamed, hulled, cracked, and then sifted. It comes in four different sizes: fine, medium, coarse, and whole. Bulgur has a very tasty, pleasant, nutty flavor to it, making it the ideal grain for this pilaf. If you can't find bulgur in your local supermarket, try a health food store.

Preparation time: *10 minutes*

Cooking time: *10 minutes under pressure*

Pressure setting: *High*

Yield: *4 to 6 servings*

2 tablespoons olive oil

1 cup whole-grain bulgur wheat, picked over

1 large red onion, chopped

2 cloves garlic, peeled and minced

2 carrots, scraped and diced small

1 stalk celery, diced small (see Figure 5-6)

8 ounces mushrooms, sliced

3 cups chicken, beef, or vegetable stock or broth

1 teaspoon salt

¼ teaspoon black pepper

1 cup cooked green peas

1 Heat the olive oil in a pressure cooker over medium-high heat. Add the bulgur wheat, onion, and garlic. Cook until the onion is soft. Add the carrots, celery, and mushrooms. Cook for 2 minutes. Add the stock, salt, and black pepper.

2 Cover and bring to high pressure over high heat. Lower the heat to stabilize the pressure. Cook for 10 minutes.

3 Remove from the heat. Let the pressure drop using a quick-release method.

4 Open and remove the cover. Taste the wheat. If it's still hard, return to Step 2 and cook for an additional 1 to 3 minutes, or until tender.

5 Fluff the pilaf. Add the peas and serve.

Per serving: Calories 208 (From Fat 54); Fat 6g (Saturated 1g); Cholesterol 9mg; Sodium 458mg; Carbohydrate 32g (Dietary Fiber 8g); Protein 9g.

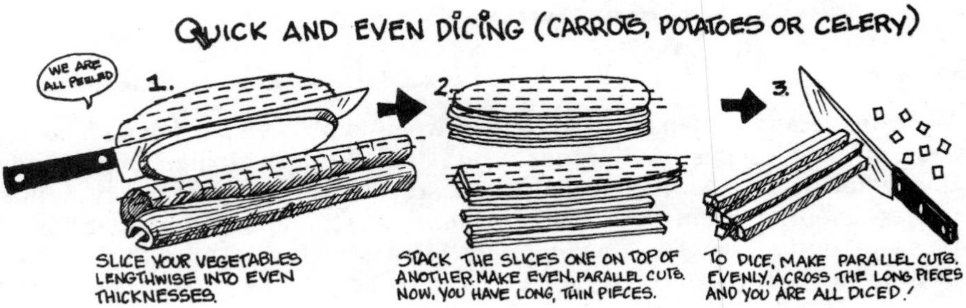

QUICK AND EVEN DICING (CARROTS, POTATOES OR CELERY)

Figure 5-6:
Dicing carrots and celery.

WE ARE ALL PEELED

1.

SLICE YOUR VEGETABLES LENGTHWISE INTO EVEN THICKNESSES.

2.

STACK THE SLICES ONE ON TOP OF ANOTHER. MAKE EVEN, PARALLEL CUTS. NOW, YOU HAVE LONG, THIN PIECES.

3.

TO DICE, MAKE PARALLEL CUTS, EVENLY, ACROSS THE LONG PIECES AND YOU ARE ALL DICED!

Chapter 6

Dried Beans in the Pressure Cooker: A Match Made in Heaven!

*T*his chapter contains a lot of recipes, and rightfully so. If ever a food was created to be made in the pressure cooker, it has to be the dried bean. Beans usually require up to 2 hours of slow simmering, but by using a pressure cooker, you reduce the cooking time by well over 70 minutes, a time savings of over 70 percent!

Beans have been a food staple around the world for well over 7,000 years. With your super-rapid pressure cooker and the recipes that follow, they'll soon become a staple ingredient in your kitchen, too! To make you a convert, I give you some great, well-known, popular recipes. Some call for cooked beans that you prepare beforehand, while others start off with dried beans after they've been soaked.

Beans: A Powerhouse of Good Things

Packed with more protein than any other legume or vegetable, beans are a protein powerhouse. Fat and cholesterol-free, they are high in fiber and provide eight out of the nine amino acids essential for good health. Beans are also high in iron and calcium and are an excellent source of complex carbohydrates, which are slowly released into our body for energy. A complete source of nutrients, beans are a key dietary component in a vegetarian diet.

If beans are so good for us, why aren't we eating them every day? Unfortunately, many people consider beans to be too labor intensive to prepare, based on the fact that they must be soaked before cooking. Other people think of beans as "un-chic." Yet, as a plant product, beans have sustained the poor of the world for thousands of years. As people and countries become more affluent, bean consumption as a source of protein diminishes, only to be replaced by meat. In the 1960s, bean consumption in the United States was 7½ pounds a person, only to decline to 5 pounds in 1984. That trend may be reversing, however. Because people today are much more aware of the importance of a balanced diet, including the need for fiber, beans are beginning to once again play an important role in people's food choices. See Figure 6-1 for the many types of beans from which to choose.

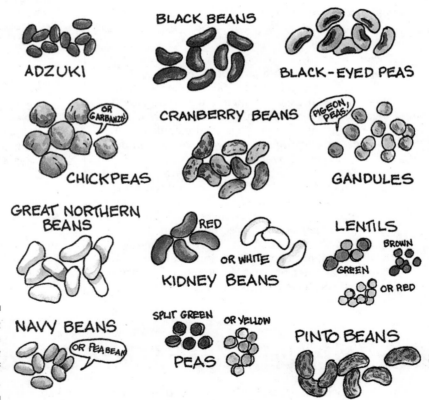

Figure 6-1: There are many varieties of beans.

"Dried" Doesn't Mean "All Dried Up"

All beans grow enclosed in a pod. Some are picked when they're still "green" or fresh. Others are picked after they've dried on the plant. Regardless, for easy and long-term storage, most beans are dried and then packaged to be sold.

Because dried beans have all the water removed from them, they won't rot and spoil. This doesn't mean that they'll last forever. Dried beans less than a year old cook better than older ones. They'll hydrate quicker and be more tender; old beans just never seem to get tender enough. Most companies don't put an expiration date on the package, so I recommend that you buy your beans either in bulk from a retailer who sells them loose by the pound or at a supermarket that has a high turnover.

A good indicator as to whether the dried beans are fresh is their appearance. They should be well shaped and not shriveled, always whole and never cracked. They should also be bright in color and shiny. If not, purchase them elsewhere.

To Soak or Not to Soak? That Is the Question

There are many theories about whether, and for how long, dried beans should be soaked before cooking. Soaking beans gets them hydrating sooner. Because you can never be certain how old the beans are, always soak them before cooking for the best results and to sort of give them a jump-start. I share with you the two most commonly used soaking methods. Regardless of the method used, always pick through the beans to remove any foreign particles, such as pebbles, dirt, or twigs, and then rinse in a colander with cold water.

Overnight soak

Use this method if you want beans the next day. Place the beans in a large bowl. Pour in enough room-temperature water so that the beans are covered by about 2 inches. Let sit overnight. Drain the beans and cook.

Are beans really a musical food?

Some people avoid eating beans because it gives them flatulence, commonly referred to as gas. Beans contain oligosaccharides. Because the human digestive system lacks an enzyme necessary to break down the oligosaccharides, they pass through our intestines undigested, only to eventually ferment and produce gas.

Oligosaccharides leach out into the water when soaking the beans, so this is another good reason to soak your beans! I recommend discarding the water used to soak them and using fresh water when you're ready to cook them.

People whose diets are high in fiber also seem to suffer less from flatulence when eating beans than those whose diets are low in fiber. Because beans are a good source of fiber, the more you eat them, the less you'll probably suffer from gas.

You also can take some over-the-counter remedies to render the oligosaccharides harmless. Some of these products are taken before eating beans, while others are added to them. The pharmacist at your local pharmacy can help you locate these remedies.

Quick soak

Place the beans in a pressure cooker or other large pot. Add enough water to cover the beans by 2 inches. Bring the water to a boil over high heat. Boil as you normally would boil water, not under pressure. Boil for 2 minutes. Remove from the heat and let sit for 1 hour to hydrate. Drain the beans and cook.

Cooking Beans

Because all beans are different, even within the same type, providing exact cooking times is difficult. (For approximate cooking times, see Table 6-1.) The times provided in the recipes are also approximate, based on my years of experience. Type, brand, and their age will determine how long the beans need to cook. If the beans are still not tender, simply cook a couple minutes longer under pressure until you're satisfied.

The following cooking times begin when the pressure cooker reaches high pressure. Always start with the shortest cooking time; you can always continue cooking under pressure for an additional couple minutes until the desired texture is reached. *Note:* With the exception of lentils and split peas, the cooking times given are for cooking *presoaked* beans.

Table 6-1	Recommended Pressure Cooker Cooking Times for Dried Beans and Legumes	
Food	**Cooking Time (in Minutes)**	**Your Notes**
Azuki beans	9 to 13	
Black beans	13 to 15	
Black-eyed peas	9 to 11	
Chickpeas (garbanzos)	20 to 25	
Cranberry beans	15 to 20	
Gandules (pigeon peas)	15 to 17	
Great Northern beans	12 to 15	
Kidney beans, red or white	12 to 15	
Lentils, green, brown, or red	8 to 10	
Navy or pea beans	10 to 12	
Peas, split green or yellow	8 to 10	
Pinto beans	8 to 10	

Beans have a tendency to foam when cooking. Therefore, never fill the pressure cooker more than half full when cooking dried beans.

You can add a tablespoon of oil to the water to reduce the foaming that beans often cause.

I recommend using the cold water release method (see Chapter 2) when the beans are done cooking. This method eliminates sputtering and foaming of cooking liquid out of the pressure regulator valve or vent pipe, which may occur if you use a quick-release method.

Never add salt to the soaking or cooking water when initially preparing beans. Salt inhibits the ability of the skin to soften, making for a tough, not too tender bean. Always season the beans after they're done cooking. Like little sponges, they'll absorb the salt quite quickly and be flavorful.

A Potful of Beans Is a Cook's Best Friend

Beans can be used in preparing all types of dishes, including dips, soups, stews, and chili.

Even though beans are available in cans, I prefer cooked, dried beans whenever possible. To save time, however, beans can be prepared beforehand and used when needed. For example, cook up a pound or two, season with salt, and store them in their cooking liquid in the fridge for up to a week.

To get you started, I provide two Master Bean recipes for cooking beans in the pressure cooker. I also give you 11 quick and easy non-pressure-cooker recipes that call for 2 to 4 cups cooked beans made from one or the other of the Master Bean recipes. Table 6-2 tells you approximately how many cups of cooked beans you can expect to get for each cup of dried beans that you cook. A good general rule when cooking dried, soaked beans is to use 2 cups of water for each cup of dried beans.

Table 6-2	Dried Beans and Legumes Cooked Yields	
Food	*Uncooked (Cups)*	*Cooked (Cups)*
Azuki beans	1	2
Black beans	1	2
Black-eyed peas	1	2¼
Chickpeas (garbanzos)	1	2½
Cranberry beans	1	2¼
Gandules (pigeon peas)	1	3
Great Northern beans	1	2¼
Kidney beans, red or white	1	2
Lentils, green, brown, or red	1	2
Navy or pea beans	1	2
Peas, split green or yellow	1	2
Pinto beans	1	2¼

↻ *Master Bean Recipe*

Beans are a cook's best friend and the best convenience food I know. A batch of cooked beans in the refrigerator means that dinner's just minutes away from being served. So cook up a batch today, use some, and refrigerate the rest to use within the next 3 to 4 days in another recipe.

Preparation time: *5 minutes, plus bean presoaking time*

Cooking time: *12 minutes under pressure*

Pressure level: *High*

Yield: *About 4 to 5 cups*

2 cups (1 pound) dried white or red kidney beans, pinto beans, or black beans, picked over

1 medium onion, whole, peeled

1 clove garlic, peeled

½ green bell pepper, cored, seeded, and cut in half

1 bay leaf

4 cups water

Salt to taste

1 Rinse the beans in a colander under cold water. Soak them, using either the overnight soak or quick soak method discussed earlier in this chapter.

2 Place the beans in a pressure cooker. Add the onion, garlic, green bell pepper, bay leaves, and water.

3 Cover and bring to high pressure over high heat. Lower the heat to stabilize pressure. Cook for 12 minutes.

4 Remove from the heat. Release the pressure with a cold-water release method.

5 Unlock and remove the cover. Taste the beans. If they're still hard, return to Step 3 and cook for an additional 2 to 4 minutes, or until tender.

6 Remove and discard the onion, garlic, green bell pepper, and bay leaf. Season with salt.

7 Use the beans to prepare any of the following recipes: Tuscan Bean Salad, Pasta Fazool, Italian Sausages and Beans, Black Beans and Rice, Refried Beans, and Prairie Fire Bean Dip. Store leftover beans in their cooking liquid, in a covered container in the refrigerator, up to four days.

Per serving: Calories 142 (From Fat 0); Fat 0g (Saturated 0g); Cholesterol 0mg; Sodium 78mg; Carbohydrate 26g (Dietary Fiber11g); Protein 10g.

☙ *Tuscan Bean Salad*

This is the perfect salad to serve with grilled meat, chicken, or fish. Be sure that the garlic is fried until golden and crisp but not burnt, or it will turn bitter. The contrast of flavors and textures — the soft, creamy beans; the crisp garlic; the crunchy celery; and its licorice-flavored leaves — makes this salad even more amazing.

Preparation time: *15 minutes*

Yield: *4 servings*

Center heart of a bunch of celery, light yellow part only, with leaves

4 cups cooked white kidney beans, cooled to room temperature

1 pint cherry or grape tomatoes

4 tablespoons olive oil

5 large cloves garlic, peeled and very thinly sliced

4 tablespoons sherry or red wine vinegar

1 teaspoon dried oregano, crumbled

Salt and pepper to taste

Boston or leaf lettuce

1 Remove all the pale yellow leaves from the celery ribs and finely mince. Slice the celery into thin pieces. Place in a large mixing bowl with the cooked beans and tomatoes. Set aside.

2 Heat the olive oil in a small skillet over medium heat. Add the garlic. Cook until golden brown and crisp, taking care not to burn. Pour over the beans and tomatoes.

3 Add the vinegar and oregano. Toss well. Season with the salt and pepper.

4 Line a serving plate with a few lettuce leaves. Spoon the bean salad on top of the lettuce and serve.

Per serving: Calories 370 (From Fat 132); Fat 15g (Saturated 2g); Cholesterol 0mg; Sodium 176mg; Carbohydrate 47g (Dietary Fiber 13g); Protein 16g.

Pasta Fazool

Immortalized by Dean Martin in his classic song *That's Amore*, pasta fazool is actually macaroni and beans or, as they properly call it in Italy, pasta e fagioli.

Preparation time: *10 minutes*

Cooking time: *4 minutes*

Yield: *4 servings*

3 tablespoons olive oil	*¼ teaspoon pepper*
1 small onion, chopped	*2 cups cooked white kidney or pinto beans*
1 clove garlic, crushed	*4 cups chicken stock*
1 plum tomato, fresh or canned, coarsely chopped	*Salt and pepper to taste*
1 carrot, diced small	*8 ounces dried ditalini (small, tube-shaped pasta), cooked al dente*
1 stalk celery, diced small	*Extra-virgin olive oil and grated pecorino Romano or Parmesan cheese for serving*
1 teaspoon dried oregano	
1½ teaspoons salt	

_1_ Heat the olive oil in a pressure cooker over medium-high heat. Add the onion and garlic. Cook until the onion is soft. Add the tomato, carrot, celery, oregano, 1½ teaspoons salt, and ¼ teaspoon pepper. Cook for 2 minutes. Add the kidney beans and stock. Stir well.

_2_ Cover and bring to high pressure over high heat. Lower the heat to stabilize the pressure. Cook for 4 minutes.

_3_ Remove from the heat. Release the pressure with a quick-release method.

_4_ Unlock and remove the cover. Season with salt and pepper.

_5_ Add the cooked ditalini (see Figure 6-2) and serve immediately.

_6_ Drizzle each serving with the olive oil. Serve with the cheese.

Per serving: *Calories 510 (From Fat 123); Fat 14g (Saturated 2g); Cholesterol 18mg; Sodium 983mg; Carbohydrate 75g (Dietary Fiber 10g); Protein 22g.*

Figure 6-2:
Pasta goes
with beans
better than
you might
think!

Italian Sausages and Beans

Sausages and beans are the perfect combination, especially when you're short on time and hungry! For best results, use the best-quality Italian sausage available, especially one made by an Italian specialty food store.

Preparation time: *5 minutes*

Cooking time: *25 minutes*

Yield: *4 servings*

2 tablespoons olive oil

4 cloves garlic, crushed

8 links Italian sausage with fennel, sweet or hot

½ cup water

½ cup red or white wine

1 can (14½ ounces) or 2 cups diced tomatoes, coarsely chopped

4 cups cooked white kidney or pinto beans

Salt and black pepper to taste

2 tablespoons minced flat-leaf parsley

1 Heat the olive oil over medium-high heat in a deep 10- or 12-inch covered skillet. Add the garlic and cook for 1 minute. Add the sausage links. Brown on both sides. Prick the sausage links with a fork. Add the water. Cover and cook for 5 to 8 minutes, or until the sausage is no longer pink in the center. Remove the cover and cook over high heat until the water evaporates.

2 Add the wine and cook for 1 minute over medium heat. Add the tomatoes and beans. Cover and cook for 15 minutes. Season with salt and pepper. Sprinkle with the parsley before serving.

Per serving: Calories 498 (From Fat 203); Fat 23g (Saturated 6g); Cholesterol 45mg; Sodium 814mg; Carbohydrate 47g (Dietary Fiber 13g); Protein 28g.

Black Beans and Rice with Pickled Red Onions

Almost every Latin American country has its own rendition of this dish.

Preparation time: 5 minutes

Cooking time: 25 minutes

Yield: 4 servings

3 tablespoons olive oil

1 green bell pepper, cored, seeded, and finely chopped

1 large onion, minced

6 cloves garlic, minced

1 teaspoon ground cumin

1 teaspoon dried oregano

4 cups cooked black beans

2 cups chicken broth

Salt and black pepper to taste

2 cups cooked white rice for serving (see Figure 6-3)

Pickled Red Onions for serving (see following recipe)

1 Heat the olive oil in a large, deep skillet over medium heat. Add the green bell pepper, onion, and garlic and cook until soft. Add the ground cumin and oregano and cook for 1 minute longer.

2 Add the beans and chicken broth. Lower the heat to a simmer and cook, covered, for 15 minutes. Mash some of the beans against the side of the skillet to thicken the cooking liquid. Season with salt and pepper.

3 Serve over the white rice. Spoon some of the pickled red onions on top of the beans.

Pickled Red Onions

Preparation time: 10 minutes

Yield: About 1½ cups

1 large red onion, cut in half and very thinly sliced

Juice from 2 fresh limes

3 tablespoons olive oil

4 sprigs cilantro, leaves only, coarsely chopped

Salt and pepper to taste

1 Combine the onion, lime juice, olive oil, and cilantro leaves in a small serving bowl. Season with salt and black pepper. Let sit at room temperature for at least 30 minutes before serving.

Per serving: Calories 529 (From Fat 168); Fat 19g (Saturated 3g); Cholesterol 3mg; Sodium 724mg; Carbohydrate 73g (Dietary Fiber 17g); Protein 19g.

Figure 6-3:
Rice is easy
to make.

How to Make Rice

so easy!

Measure the rice and water. Put them into the pot. Add salt and butter (optional).

Bring to a boil. Stir once. Reduce heat to a simmer. Cover the pot.

Rice is DONE when all the liquid is absorbed. You can see little steam holes on the surface of the rice.

☕ Refried Beans

Most recipes for refried beans are made with lard. I found olive oil to be a good, healthy substitute. Serve these beans as a side dish or use them to make Prairie Fire Bean Dip or Bean Burritos with Fresh Tomato Salsa, recipes that you can find later in this chapter.

Preparation time: *5 minutes*

Cooking time: *15 minutes*

Yield: *About 3 cups*

2 tablespoons olive oil

1 large onion, minced

1 clove garlic, minced

4 cups cooked red kidney or pinto beans, drained, 1 cup cooking liquid reserved

1 teaspoon dried marjoram leaves

Salt and pepper to taste

1 Heat the oil over medium-high heat in a large skillet. Add the onion and garlic and cook until soft.

2 Add the beans, marjoram, and ½ cup of the cooking liquid. Over low heat, begin to gently mash the beans with the back of a large kitchen spoon or potato masher. Continue cooking, stirring continuously, until you obtain a thick, somewhat creamy mixture that begins to pull away from the sides of the pan. If the mixture appears too dry, add additional cooking liquid, a couple tablespoons at a time.

3 Season with salt and pepper.

Per serving: Calories 151 (From Fat 35); Fat 4g (Saturated 1g); Cholesterol 0mg; Sodium 2mg; Carbohydrate 22g (Dietary Fiber 6g); Protein 8g.

⌖ *Prairie Fire Bean Dip*

Serve this spicy, refried bean dip with tortilla chips or crackers. The provolone or Asiago cheese adds an interesting flavor. If you prefer a milder tasting dip, cut down on the amount of jalapeño peppers or use mild green chiles.

Preparation time: *5 minutes*

Cooking time: *15 minutes*

Yield: *About 4 cups*

4 ounces provolone or Asiago cheese, shredded

4 tablespoons butter or margarine, cut into small cubes

1 can (3½ ounces) roasted jalapeños or green chiles, chopped, 1 teaspoon juice reserved

2 tablespoons minced onion

1 clove garlic, minced

About 3 cups Refried Beans, still hot in the skillet (see recipe earlier in this chapter)

1 Add the cheese, butter, chiles, onion, and garlic to the refried beans.

2 Cook over low heat, stirring continuously until the cheese and butter are melted.

3 Serve dip hot with tortilla chips or crackers.

Per serving: *Calories 170 (From Fat 80); Fat 9g (Saturated 4g); Cholesterol 17mg; Sodium 182mg; Carbohydrate 16g (Dietary Fiber 4g); Protein 8g.*

☙ Bean Burritos with Fresh Tomato Salsa

Bean burritos freeze well when wrapped in foil. To reheat, just pop them in the oven frozen and bake until they're hot and the cheese is melted.

Preparation time: *10 minutes*

Cooking time: *15 to 20 minutes*

Yield: *6 burritos*

About 3 cups Refried Beans (see recipe earlier in this chapter)

Six 10-inch flour tortillas

1¼ cups shredded sharp cheddar cheese

Pickled jalapeño slices (optional, available in jars at most supermarkets)

Fresh Tomato Salsa (see following recipe)

Sour cream (optional)

1 Preheat the oven to 400°. Spoon approximately ½ cup refried beans down one-third of a tortilla, 1 inch from the top and bottom edges. Sprinkle with 2 tablespoons of cheese and a couple jalapeño slices, if desired.

2 Fold up about 1 inch of the bottom and the top of the tortilla over the filling. Roll the filling into the tortilla. (See Figure 6-4.) Place the burritos on a baking pan. Cover with foil and bake until the filling is heated through and the cheese melts, approximately 15 to 20 minutes.

3 Carefully remove with a spatula to serving plates. Serve with Fresh Tomato Salsa or, if desired, the sour cream.

Fresh Tomato Salsa

Preparation time: *5 minutes*

Yield: *About 1½ cups*

2 large ripe tomatoes, cut into eighths

2 scallions, white and light green parts only, cut into eighths

2 cloves garlic, peeled and quartered

8 sprigs cilantro, leaves only

1 tablespoon freshly squeezed lime juice

Salt to taste

Hot pepper sauce to taste

1 Place the tomatoes, scallions, garlic, cilantro, and lime juice in a food processor bowl or blender jar. Pulse 2 or 3 times until finely chopped. Do not puree.

2 Season with salt and hot pepper sauce.

Per serving: *Calories 546 (From Fat 164); Fat 18g (Saturated 7g); Cholesterol 25mg; Sodium 494mg; Carbohydrate 74g (Dietary Fiber 11g); Protein 24g.*

HOW TO ROLL A BURRITO

1. SPOON APPROXIMATELY ½ CUP OF REFRIED BEANS DOWN ⅓ OF A (12") TORTILLA, 1" FROM THE TOP AND BOTTOM EDGES.

2. SPRINKLE WITH 2 TABLESPOONS OF CHEESE AND A COUPLE OF JALAPENO SLICES IF DESIRED.

3. FOLD UP ABOUT 1" OF THE BOTTOM AND TOP OF THE TORTILLA, OVER THE FILLING.

4. ROLL THE FILLING INTO THE TORTILLA.

5. PLACE BURRITOS ON A BAKING PAN. COVER WITH FOIL. BAKE UNTIL FILLING IS HEATED THROUGH, CHEESE MELTS, ABOUT 15-20 MINUTES.

WE'RE HOT!

Figure 6-4: Rolling and folding burritos.

🍅 Black Beans and Vegetable Soup

This is my version of the classic black bean soup, the main difference being the addition of chunky vegetables to the creamy bean broth. As with most soups, this one tastes better the next day, after it has had a chance to sit.

Preparation time: *10 minutes, plus bean presoaking time*

Cooking time: *24 minutes under pressure*

Pressure level: *High*

Yield: *6 to 8 servings*

2 cups (1 pound) black beans, picked over	*1 can (14½ ounces) diced tomatoes*
2 tablespoons olive oil	*1 bay leaf*
1 large onion, chopped	*7 cups chicken broth or water*
2 cloves garlic, minced	*3 carrots, diced*
1 red bell pepper, cored, seeded, and diced small (see Figure 6-5)	*2 stalks celery, diced*
1 teaspoon ground cumin	*1 cup fresh or frozen corn kernels*
1 teaspoon paprika	*Salt and black pepper to taste*
1 teaspoon dried oregano	*Sour cream for serving (optional)*

1 Rinse the beans in a colander under cold water. Soak the beans, using either the overnight soak or the quick soak method, discussed earlier in this chapter.

2 Heat the olive oil in a pressure cooker over medium-high heat. Add the onion, garlic, and red bell pepper. Cook until the onion is soft. Add the ground cumin, paprika, and oregano. Cook for 1 minute. Add the tomatoes and cook for 2 minutes. Add the beans, bay leaf, and chicken broth.

3 Cover and bring to high pressure over high heat. Lower the heat to stabilize pressure. Cook for 20 minutes.

4 Remove from the heat. Release the pressure with a quick-release method.

5 Unlock and remove the cover. Taste the beans. If they're still hard, return to Step 3 and cook them for an additional 2 to 3 minutes.

6 Remove and discard the bay leaf. Remove 4 cups of cooked beans with broth and puree in a blender. Return to the pressure cooker. Season with the salt and pepper. Add the carrots, celery, and corn. Cover and bring to high pressure over high heat. Lower the heat to stabilize the pressure. Cook for 4 minutes.

7 Remove from the heat. Release the pressure with a quick-release method. Unlock and remove the cover. Season with the salt and black pepper. If desired, serve with a dollop of sour cream.

Per serving: Calories 280 (From Fat 70); Fat 8g (Saturated 2g); Cholesterol 4mg; Sodium 1,272mg; Carbohydrate 41g (Dietary Fiber 14g); Protein 13g.

How to Core and Seed a Pepper

Figure 6-5: Coring, seeding, and dicing bell peppers.

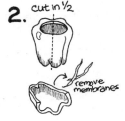

1. cut out stem / twist and pull out

2. cut in ½ / remove membranes

3. Cut into lengthwise strips

4. For cubes, hold strips together and cut crosswise

Senate Bean Soup

No one is exactly certain as to the origin of this soup. We do know, however, that it's been on the menus of the U.S. Senate and House restaurants on Capitol Hill for more than 40 years. Usually slow simmered for over 4 hours with a smoked ham hock (the lower portion of a hog's hind leg), this bean soup is my speedier, pressure cooker version. You can find ham hocks in the refrigerated meat case at your local supermarket, usually with the other pork products.

Preparation time: *15 minutes, plus bean presoaking time*

Cooking time: *15 minutes under pressure*

Pressure level: *High*

Yield: *About 4 cups*

1 pound navy beans, picked over	*1 carrot, peeled and chopped*
2 tablespoons vegetable oil	*1 stalk celery, chopped*
1 large onion, chopped	*6 cups water*
1 smoked ham hock	*Salt and pepper to taste*

1 Rinse the beans in a colander under cold water. Soak the beans, using either the overnight soak or quick soak method.

2 Heat the vegetable oil in a pressure cooker over medium-high heat. Add the onion and and cook until soft and golden brown. Add the beans, ham hock, carrot, celery, and water.

3 Cover and bring to high pressure over high heat. Lower the heat to stabilize the pressure. Cook for 15 minutes.

4 Remove from the heat. Release the pressure with a quick-release method.

5 Unlock and remove the cover. Taste the beans. If they're still hard, return to Step 3 and cook them for 2 to 3 minutes longer.

6 Remove the skin and meat from the ham hock. Discard the skin and bones. Chop up the meat and add to the beans.

7 Roughly mash the beans with a potato masher until the soup is thick but lumpy. Season with salt and pepper.

Per serving: *Calories 287 (From Fat 76); Fat 8g (Saturated 2g); Cholesterol 20mg; Sodium 102mg; Carbohydrate 37g (Dietary Fiber 9g); Protein 17g.*

☙ Drunken Beans

These are the type of beans you would expect to eat while sitting around a campfire during a cattle roundup out on the trail. You'll be surprised how good they can also taste when eaten in your own backyard with barbecued meat or poultry!

Preparation time: *5 minutes, plus bean presoaking time*

Cooking time: *20 minutes under pressure*

Pressure level: *High*

Yield: *6 to 8 servings*

2 cups (1 pound) dried black or pinto beans, picked over

1 large onion, chopped

2 cloves garlic, minced

2½ cups water

1 can (12 ounces) beer

1 can (14½ ounces) Mexican-style diced tomatoes with jalapeño

1 tablespoon chili powder

3 teaspoons ground cumin

2 teaspoons salt

½ cup prepared barbecue sauce

Salt to taste

1 Rinse the beans in a colander under cold water. Soak them, using either the overnight soak or the quick soak method, discussed earlier in this chapter.

2 Place the beans in a pressure cooker. Add the onion, garlic, water, and beer.

3 Cover and bring to high pressure over high heat. Lower the heat to stabilize the pressure. Cook for 15 minutes.

4 Remove from the heat. Release the pressure with a quick-release method.

5 Unlock and remove the cover. Taste the beans. If they're still hard, return to Step 3 and cook the beans for an additional 2 to 3 minutes.

6 Add the tomatoes, chili powder, ground cumin, salt, and barbecue sauce.

7 Cover and bring to high pressure over high heat. Lower the heat to stabilize the pressure. Cook for 5 minutes. Remove from the heat. Release the pressure with a quick-release method.

8 Unlock and remove the cover. Mash some of the beans against the side of the pressure cooker to thicken the cooking liquid. Season with salt.

Per serving: Calories 195 (From Fat 10); Fat 1g (Saturated 0g); Cholesterol 0mg; Sodium 854mg; Carbohydrate 36g (Dietary Fiber 12g); Protein 12g.

N'awlins Red Beans and Rice

Simple and humble, red beans and rice is probably the most famous of the prized culinary creations in New Orleans. There are as many variations of red beans and rice as there are cooks.

Preparation time: *15 minutes, plus bean presoaking time*

Cooking time: *16 minutes under pressure*

Pressure level: *High*

Yield: *8 servings*

2 cups (1 pound) dried red kidney beans, picked over

2 tablespoons olive oil

1 large onion, chopped

4 cloves garlic, minced

2 carrots, peeled and finely chopped

2 stalks celery, finely chopped

1 can (14½ ounces) diced tomatoes

1 teaspoon Tabasco Sauce

1 bay leaf

1 smoked ham hock

4 cups water

Salt and pepper to taste

½ pound smoked andouille sausage or smoked kielbasa, thinly sliced

3 cups cooked white rice for serving

1 Rinse the beans in a colander under cold water. Soak them, using either the overnight soak or quick soak method, discussed earlier in this chapter.

2 Heat the olive oil in a pressure cooker over medium-high heat. Add the onion and garlic. Cook until the onion is soft. Add the carrots, celery, tomatoes, Tabasco Sauce, and bay leaf. Cook for 2 minutes. Add the beans, ham hock, and water.

3 Cover and bring to high pressure over high heat. Lower the heat to stabilize the pressure. Cook for 15 minutes.

4 Remove from the heat. Release pressure with a quick-release method.

5 Unlock and remove the cover. Taste the beans. If they're still hard, return to Step 3 and cook them for an additional 2 to 3 minutes.

6 Season with salt and pepper. Add the sausage. Cover and bring to high pressure over high heat. Lower the heat to stabilize pressure. Cook for 1 minute. Remove from the heat. Release pressure with a quick-release method.

7 Unlock and remove the cover. Remove the skin and meat from the ham hock. Discard the skin and bone. Chop the meat and add to the beans. Remove and discard the bay leaf. Mash some of the beans with a spoon against the side of the pressure cooker to thicken the cooking liquid. Season with salt and pepper. Serve with the white rice.

Per serving: *Calories 425 (From Fat 16); Fat 5g (Saturated 5g); Cholesterol 39mg; Sodium 489mg; Carbohydrate 50g (Dietary Fiber 9g); Protein 21g.*

Tailgate Chili

My favorite chili has not only great flavor but also fantastic color. The color comes from a combination of green peppers, red peppers, and bright orange carrots, a secret ingredient that mellows the jalapeño heat.

Preparation time: *25 minutes, plus bean presoaking time*

Cooking time: *15 minutes under pressure*

Pressure setting: *High*

Yield: *8 to 10 servings*

2 cups (1 pound) pinto beans, picked over

3 tablespoons olive oil

1 large onion, chopped

2 cloves garlic, minced

1 large green bell pepper, cored, seeded, and chopped

1 large red bell pepper, cored, seeded, and chopped

1 jalapeño pepper, cored, seeded, and chopped

2 carrots, peeled and chopped

2 stalks celery, chopped

2 tablespoons chili powder

4 teaspoons ground cumin

1 teaspoon ground oregano

1 pound lean ground beef

1 can (28 ounces) crushed tomatoes

1¾ cups water

Salt to taste

3 cups cooked white rice for serving

Shredded cheddar cheese for serving

1 Rinse the beans in a colander under cold water. Soak them, using either the overnight soak or quick soak method, discussed earlier in this chapter.

2 Heat the olive oil in a pressure cooker over medium-high heat. Add the onion; garlic; green, red, and jalapeño peppers; carrots; and celery. Cook until the onion is soft. Add the chili powder, cumin, and oregano. Stir and cook for 1 minute. Add the ground beef and cook until no longer pink, breaking up large chunks with a spoon. Add the tomatoes, beans, and water. Stir to combine.

3 Cover and bring to high pressure over high heat. Lower the heat to stabilize pressure. Cook for 15 minutes.

4 Remove from the heat. Release the pressure with a quick-release method.

5 Unlock and remove the cover. Taste the beans. If they're still hard, return to Step 3 and cook them for an additional 2 to 3 minutes.

6 Season with salt. Serve over the white rice and garnish with the cheddar cheese.

Per serving: *Calories 462 (From Fat 116); Fat 13g (Saturated 3g); Cholesterol 41mg; Sodium 276mg; Carbohydrate 63g (Dietary Fiber 15g); Protein 26g. (cheese not included)*

ᦐ *Master Chickpea Recipe*

Chickpeas have been a dietary staple for more than 7,000 years. Originally grown in Asia, they were spread throughout the Mediterranean region by the Phoenicians and brought to the Americas by the Spanish. These round, golden beans maintain their shape well when cooked and are a favorite in soups, stews, salads, and dips, so it's well worth having a batch on hand in the refrigerator.

Preparation time: *5 minutes, plus bean presoaking time*

Cooking time: *25 minutes under pressure*

Pressure level: *High*

Yield: *About 5 cups*

2 cups (1 pound) dried chickpeas, picked over

1 medium onion, peeled, stuck with 6 dried cloves

2 cloves garlic, peeled

1 bay leaf

4 cups water

Salt to taste

1 Rinse the chickpeas in a colander under cold water. Soak the beans, using either the overnight soak or quick soak method, discussed earlier in this chapter.

2 Place the chickpeas in a pressure cooker. Add the onion, garlic, bay leaf, and water.

3 Cover and bring to high pressure over high heat. Lower the heat to stabilize the pressure. Cook for 25 minutes.

4 Remove from the heat. Release pressure with the cold-water release method. Taste the beans. If they're still hard, return to Step 3 and cook them for an additional 2 to 3 minutes.

5 Remove and discard the onion, garlic, and bay leaf. Season with salt.

6 Use the chickpeas to prepare the Spicy Indian Chickpea Stew, Three-Bean Salad, Garlicky Chickpeas and Cabbage Soup, and Hummus recipes later in this chapter.

Per serving: Calories 170 (From Fat 24); Fat 3g (Saturated 0g); Cholesterol 0mg; Sodium 80mg; Carbohydrate 28g (Dietary Fiber 8g); Protein 9g.

ᕽ *Spicy Indian Chickpea Stew*

This recipe is a particular favorite of mine. I like to serve it with basmati rice on the side and a simple cucumber and radish salad.

Preparation time: *5 minutes*

Cooking time: *15 minutes*

Yield: *4 servings*

2 tablespoons olive oil	*Pinch of cayenne pepper*
1 medium onion, chopped	*2 cups cooked chickpeas*
1 clove garlic, minced	*½ teaspoon salt*
1 teaspoon ground coriander	*¼ teaspoon black pepper*
½ teaspoon ground cumin	*1 teaspoon freshly squeezed lemon juice*
⅛ teaspoon turmeric	*2 tablespoons minced cilantro*

1 Heat the olive oil in a large skillet over medium-high heat. Add the onion and garlic and cook until soft. Add the coriander, cumin, turmeric, and cayenne pepper. Cook for 1 minute.

2 Stir in the chickpeas, salt, and pepper. Cook until the chickpeas are heated through.

3 Remove from the heat and stir in the lemon juice and cilantro.

Per serving: *Calories 207 (From Fat 82); Fat 9g (Saturated 1g); Cholesterol 0mg; Sodium 298mg; Carbohydrate 25g (Dietary Fiber 7g); Protein 8g.*

☜ *Three-Bean Salad*

This classic 1950s salad tastes so much better when made with recently cooked dried beans and fresh green beans rather than canned beans. Prepare the salad the day before because the beans need to marinate overnight in the vinaigrette.

Preparation time: *5 minutes, plus marinating overnight*

Yield: *8 servings*

2 cups cooked red kidney beans

2 cups cooked chickpeas

1 pound green beans, cut into 1-inch pieces and cooked

1 small green bell pepper, cored, seeded, and finely chopped

1 small onion, finely chopped

¼ cup vegetable oil

⅓ cup white vinegar

¼ cup sugar

½ teaspoon salt

¼ teaspoon black pepper

1 Combine the kidney beans, chickpeas, green beans, green bell pepper, and onion together in a large storage container or glass jar.

2 Whisk together the vegetable oil, vinegar, sugar, salt, and black pepper.

3 Pour the vinaigrette over the beans and toss. Cover and refrigerate for 24 hours before serving.

Per serving: Calories 230(From Fat 74); Fat 8g (Saturated 1g); Cholesterol 0mg; Sodium 151mg; Carbohydrate 33g (Dietary Fiber 8g); Protein 9g.

☺ *Garlicky Chickpeas and Cabbage Soup*

I learned to make this Spanish soup, or *portaje,* when I lived in Spain. In fact, it was the first thing I learned to cook in the pressure cooker over 20 years ago and still remains a personal favorite.

Preparation time: *10 minutes*

Cooking time: *6 minutes under pressure*

Pressure level: *High*

Yield: *6 to 8 servings*

3 tablespoons olive oil	*1 can (15 ounces) tomato sauce*
8 cloves garlic, minced	*3 cups water*
4 cups shredded, cored green cabbage (see Figure 6-6)	*1 teaspoon salt*
	¼ teaspoon pepper
4 cups cooked chickpeas	*Salt and pepper to taste*

1 Heat the olive oil in a pressure cooker over medium heat. Add the garlic and cook for 1 to 2 minutes or until golden. Add the cabbage and cook for 5 minutes. Add the chickpeas, tomato sauce, water, salt, and pepper.

2 Cover and bring to high pressure over high heat. Lower the heat to stabilize the pressure. Cook for 6 minutes.

3 Remove from the heat. Release the pressure with a quick-release method.

4 Unlock and remove the cover. Season with salt and pepper.

Per serving: *Calories 211 (From Fat 67); Fat 7g (Saturated 1g); Cholesterol 0mg; Sodium 627mg; Carbohydrate 30g (Dietary Fiber 8g); Protein 9g.*

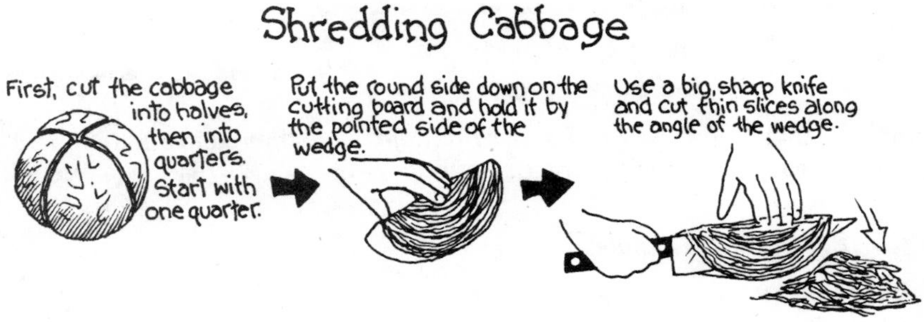

Shredding Cabbage

Figure 6-6:
How to
shred a
cabbage.

First, cut the cabbage into halves, then into quarters. Start with one quarter.

Put the round side down on the cutting board and hold it by the pointed side of the wedge.

Use a big, sharp knife and cut thin slices along the angle of the wedge.

 Hummus

Hummus is a delicious, flavorful Middle Eastern appetizer that can be served with toasted pita triangles, French bread, or vegetable crudités. Or make pita pocket sandwiches by filling the pitas with hummus, chopped tomatoes, and shredded lettuce.

Preparation time: *5 minutes*

Yield: *About 2 cups*

2 cups cooked chickpeas	1 teaspoon salt
4 tablespoons olive oil	1 clove garlic, quartered
3 tablespoons freshly squeezed lemon juice	½ cup flat-leaf parsley, leaves only

1 Place all the ingredients in a food processor bowl.

2 Process until smooth, scraping down the sides of the bowl. Add additional lemon juice if the hummus is too thick.

Per serving: Calories 130 (From Fat 70); Fat 8g (Saturated 1g); Cholesterol 12mg; Sodium 295mg; Carbohydrate 12g (Dietary Fiber 3g); Protein 4g.

Chapter 7

Roasts and Poultry

In This Chapter

▶ Obtaining maximum flavor with minimum effort

▶ Choosing the right cuts for the pressure cooker

▶ Making use of the steaming basket

▶ Knowing when the meat is done

▶ Cooking a roast for any occasion

Roasts and large cuts of meat and poultry are usually reserved for occasions such as a family celebration, the holidays, or a leisurely Sunday dinner around the table with family and friends. Roasts are an easy way to feed a group of people, but they also take two to three hours to cook. The long cooking time may be the real reason why they're served only occasionally. That's too bad, because my favorite part of a roast is the delicious leftovers enjoyed the next day!

Fabulous Results in Half the Time

A few years ago, I decided to try my hand at adapting a basic, favorite pot roast recipe for the pressure cooker. First, I made sure that the meat would fit comfortably in the pressure cooker, which is about 8½ inches in diameter. I determined that a 3- to 3½-pound roast would be perfect. Because I already knew that the pressure cooker tenderizes as it cooks, I purchased an inexpensive cut of beef, a rump roast from the hindquarters.

I followed the original recipe by generously seasoning the meat with salt and freshly ground black pepper. I then browned and seared it in the pressure cooker over high heat to seal in the juices. To build on the flavor, I added some onion, which I cooked quickly for a minute or two. With all of these great caramelized flavors on the bottom of the pot, I added some red wine to deglaze and scrape up any cooked-on particles. I then increased the liquid with some homemade beef broth. I didn't really want the meat to boil, so I placed it in a steaming basket on top of a trivet in the pressure cooker. The moment of truth came about an hour later, about 90 minutes less than it would have normally taken, when I opened the pressure cooker and cut into the meat. The meat was fork-tender and succulent! The gravy, ambrosial!

I was then inspired to try other cuts of meat, such as pork loin, quartered chicken, and, yes, even a whole turkey breast, all of which cooked perfectly in my pressure cooker. Before I knew it, come mealtime, every day was like Sunday!

Not All Cuts Are Created Equal

Some cuts of meat are better suited for cooking in the pressure cooker than others, especially, tougher, less expensive ones and cuts that are very lean, because they cook up tender under pressure. A basic cooking method for preparing large cuts of meats and poultry is braising. When you braise, you first brown the food over medium-high heat in a small amount of oil. The browned food is then cooked, covered, over low heat in a small amount of cooking liquid for an extended period of time until it is fork tender.

The following are some suggestions of different cuts of meats and poultry that I particularly like to make in the pressure cooker.

Beef

All cuts of beef (see Figure 7-1) that come from the front and hind quarters are ideal for the pressure cooker because there is lots of developed muscle here from lumbering around, and not much fat. Some good choices are chuck and brisket from the front of the steer, and round and rump, well, from the rump or rear of the animal. Other good choices are flank and skirt steak from the belly area.

Pork

Pork really is the other white meat. Much leaner today than ever before, it can also dry out quickly when cooked. The loin is very lean white meat and is ideal for roasting and braising in the pressure cooker. To maximize flavor and to ensure that the pork is juicy, I like to rub it with a paste of garlic and spices before browning it on all sides in the pressure cooker in a small amount of oil. Lots of vegetables and some cooking liquid are sure to keep the meat tender.

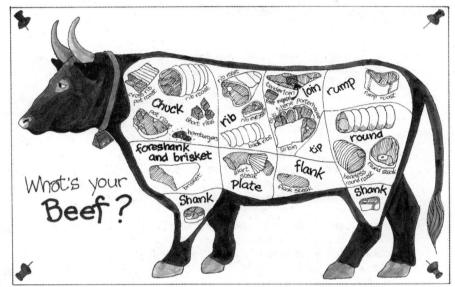

Figure 7-1:
Popular cuts of meat and where they come from.

Lamb

A boneless, tied leg of lamb, stuffed with pieces of garlic and rosemary, browned in olive oil, and braised with dry white wine, is a superb piece of meat for the pressure cooker, especially when company is coming and you want to impress your guests. Less expensive lamb shanks are also delectable when braised in the pressure cooker, too, with the now tender meat falling off the bone.

Poultry

From a cook's standpoint, chickens and turkeys are poorly designed creatures. It's almost impossible to get a whole bird, with its juicier dark meat and drier white meat, to cook evenly without something coming out dry and stringy. But when made in the pressure cooker, chicken, whole or quartered, comes out succulent. Although you may not be able to fit a whole turkey into even an 8-quart pressure cooker, a 4- to 5-pound whole breast fits perfectly in a 6-quart pressure cooker and cooks up juicy, as do turkey legs and wings.

Using Steaming Baskets for Roasts

Some pressure cookers include steaming baskets or racks (see Chapter 2). A steaming basket is made of metal and is usually about 7 inches in diameter and 2 to 3 inches deep, with small round cutouts along the bottom, for, well, steaming. The basket usually comes with a metal wire trivet. The trivet is placed in the pressure cooker first and the basket on top. Other pressure cookers come with a steaming rack. This accessory looks like a 7-inch diameter lid with small round cutouts on top. It sits directly in the pressure cooker. Steaming baskets and racks serve the same purpose: to keep the food out of contact with the cooking liquid. When braising large cuts of meat such as chuck and rump roasts and boneless legs of lamb in the pressure cooker, I have found the results to be better if the meat doesn't sit directly in the cooking liquid, where it has a tendency to boil, but rather in a steaming basket.

If your pressure cooker has none of these two steaming devices, you can always purchase an inexpensive, collapsible, metal steaming basket at any housewares store. Regardless of the type you use, the steaming basket or rack is placed in the pressure cooker after the meat is browned, and as detailed in the recipe.

Besides a steaming basket, some pressure cookers also come with an insert dish or pan. The same diameter and depth as the basket, the dish varies in that there are no holes on the bottom. They can be used to make casserole dishes and desserts.

Is It Done Yet?

For the most part, meat is roasted or braised in the pressure cooker until fork-tender. Because cooking also kills harmful bacteria, it's important that meat be cooked for the bacteria to be killed off.

An instant-read thermometer is a good way to determine whether meat or poultry is adequately cooked. Place the probe into the thickest part of the meat, inserted about halfway down without touching the bone or pot. Table 7-1 provides you with safe cooking temperatures for cooked meat and poultry.

Table 7-1	Meat and Poultry Safe Cooking Temperatures
Food	*Safe Cooking Temperature*
Beef	170° (well done)
Chicken	180°
Ground meat or poultry	165°
Ham (cured pork)	140°
Lamb	170° (well done)
Pork	160°
Turkey	180°

Table 7-2 offers recommended cooking times for meat and poultry prepared in a pressure cooker. The cooking times begin when the pressure cooker reaches high pressure. Always start with the shortest cooking time; you can always continue cooking under pressure for an additional couple minutes until the desired texture is reached. All cooking times are at best approximations and should be used as a general guideline. Not all cuts of meat cook for the same amount of time. You may also find that your particular brand or model of pressure cooker cooks faster or even a bit slower. Therefore, feel free to note any cooking time differences in the right-hand column of Table 7-2.

Table 7-2	Recommended Pressure Cooker Cooking Times for Meat and Poultry	
Food	*Cooking Time (in Minutes)*	*Your Notes*
Beef/veal, roast or brisket	50 to 60	
Beef/veal, shank, 1½ inch thick	25 to 35	
Beef, corned	50 to 60	
Lamb, boneless roast	45 to 55	
Pork, loin roast	40 to 50	
Pork, smoked butt	20 to 25	

(continued)

Table 7-2 *(continued)*		
Food	*Cooking Time (in Minutes)*	*Your Notes*
Pork, ham shank	30 to 40	
Chicken, whole	15 to 20	
Chicken, pieces	10 to 12	
Turkey, whole breast	30 to 40	

A Roast in Every Pot

The following are a few of my favorite roast recipes for the pressure cooker that I want to share with you. For the most part, they require very little preparation, and I know that you'll be pleased by how quick and easy they are to make — and delicious, too!

Sunday Pot Roast

This is the starting point for good pot roast. It's a very simple and basic recipe. You can add vegetables if you want or leave them out. Regardless, the meat always comes out tender and flavorful, with plenty of gravy for spooning over mashed potatoes or noodles.

Preparation time: 20 minutes

Cooking time: 60 minutes under pressure

Pressure level: High

Yield: 6 to 8 servings

2 tablespoons all-purpose flour

2 teaspoons salt

¼ teaspoon pepper

3- to 4-pound boneless, trimmed chuck or rump roast

1 tablespoon olive oil

1 small onion, sliced

1 bay leaf

1½ cups beef broth, red wine, water, or any combination

Salt and pepper to taste

1 Combine the flour, salt, and pepper. Rub into the roast.

2 Heat the olive oil in a pressure cooker over high heat. Add the roast and brown evenly on all sides.

3 Add the onion and cook for 1 minute. Add the bay leaf. Remove the meat to a platter or dish. Place the steaming basket in the pressure cooker. Place the browned meat in the steaming basket. Add the beef broth.

4 Cover and bring to high pressure over high heat. Lower the heat to stabilize the pressure. Cook for 60 minutes.

5 Remove from the heat. Release the pressure with a quick-release method. Unlock and remove the cover. Test the roast with a fork. The fork should penetrate easily. If not tender, cover and cook under pressure for an additional 10 minutes.

6 Remove the roast and the steaming basket. Cover and let sit for 10 minutes before slicing.

7 If the gravy isn't thick enough, bring to a boil, uncovered, and cook until reduced. Season with salt and pepper. Remove and discard the bay leaf. Slice the roast against the grain (see Figure 7-2) and serve with the gravy.

Per serving: Calories 417 (From Fat 267); Fat 30g (Saturated 11g); Cholesterol 116mg; Sodium 912mg; Carbohydrate 2g (Dietary Fiber 0g); Protein 33g.

Cutting Pot Roast Across the Grain

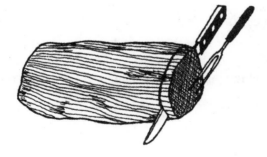

Figure 7-2:
Slicing meat across the grain.

Ropa Vieja with Fried Plantains

This two-part Latino recipe is aptly called *ropa vieja,* which means "old clothes." The meat is first cooked, or *washed,* so to speak, only to be shredded afterwards and then cooked for a second time in a rich tomato sauce as if it were "secondhand." Serve this dish with cooked white rice and fried plantains.

Preparation time: *20 minutes*

Cooking time: *50 minutes under pressure*

Pressure level: *High*

Yield: *8 servings*

1 large onion, cut into ¼-inch-thick slices

2 pounds beef brisket or flank steak, trimmed of all fat

Salt and black pepper to taste

1 carrot, peeled and cut into 1-inch pieces

1 stalk celery, cut into 1-inch pieces

1 sprig parsley

About 4 cups water

2 tablespoons olive oil

1 medium onion, chopped

2 cloves garlic, minced

1 green bell pepper, cored, seeded, and chopped

1 can (14½ ounces) tomato sauce

¼ teaspoon dried oregano

1 bay leaf

1 tablespoon red wine vinegar

3 cups cooked white rice

Fried Plantains (see following recipe)

1 Place the onion slices on the bottom of a pressure cooker, overlapping if necessary. Cut the brisket to fit flat in the pressure cooker. Generously salt and pepper the brisket. Place on top of the onion. Add the carrot, celery, and parsley. Add just enough water to cover the meat, about 4 cups.

2 Cover and bring to high pressure over high heat. Lower the heat to stabilize the pressure. Cook for 50 minutes.

3 Remove from the heat. Let the pressure drop using a quick-release method.

4 Unlock and remove the cover.

5 Remove the brisket from the cooking liquid. Discard the vegetables and strain the broth. Measure 1 cup of the broth and set aside. Shred the meat and set aside. Wash and dry the pressure cooker.

6 Heat the olive oil in the pressure cooker over medium-high heat. Add the chopped onion, garlic, and green pepper. Cook until the onion is soft. Add the tomato sauce, reserved broth, oregano, bay leaf, and vinegar. Stir in the shredded meat.

7 Cover and bring to high pressure over high heat. Lower the heat to stabilize the pressure. Cook for 5 minutes.

8 Remove from the heat. Let the pressure drop using a quick-release method.

9 Unlock and remove the cover. Season with salt and black pepper. Serve with the rice and Fried Plantains.

Per serving (with rice, without plantains): Calories 307 (From Fat 112); Fat 12g (Saturated 4g); Cholesterol 59mg; Sodium 168mg; Carbohydrate 22g (Dietary Fiber 2g); Protein 26g.

Fried Plantains

Preparation time: *10 minutes*

Cooking time: *15 minutes*

Yield: *8 servings*

Vegetable oil	*3 large very ripe plantains (black skin), peeled and cut on a diagonal into ½-inch slices*

Heat 1 inch of oil in a large skillet over medium-high heat. Fry the plantain slices in batches on both sides until deep brown. Drain on paper towels.

Per serving: Calories 127 (From Fat 48); Fat 5g (Saturated 1g); Cholesterol 0mg; Sodium 3mg; Carbohydrate 21g (Dietary Fiber 2g); Protein 1g.

"Barbecued" Beef

What could be simpler for getting delicious barbecue-style taste than braising a piece of meat in flavorful, smoky barbecue sauce? I like to serve this dish with Drunken Beans (Chapter 6) and corn on the cob. For best results, let the meat sit for at least 15 minutes before slicing thin.

Preparation time: *20 minutes*

Cooking time: *60 minutes under pressure*

Pressure level: *High*

Yield: *6 to 8 servings*

1 tablespoon vegetable oil	2 stalks celery, finely chopped
3- to 4-pound boneless, trimmed chuck or rump roast	1½ cups prepared barbecue sauce
	1 can (12 ounces) beer
1 large onion, sliced	1½ teaspoons chili powder

1 Heat the oil in a pressure cooker over medium-high heat. Add the roast and brown evenly on all sides.

2 Add the onion and celery. Cook for 1 minute. Remove the roast to a plate. Add the barbecue sauce, beer, and chili powder. Stir well. Place the steaming basket in the pressure cooker. Place the browned roast in the steaming basket.

3 Cover and bring to high pressure over high heat. Lower the heat to stabilize the pressure. Cook for 60 minutes.

4 Remove from the heat. Release the pressure using the natural-release method (see Chapter 2). When the pressure has dropped, unlock and remove the cover. Test the roast with a fork; the fork should penetrate easily. If not tender, cover and cook under pressure for an additional 10 minutes.

5 Remove the roast. Slice against the grain. Serve with the barbecue sauce.

Per serving: Calories 451 (From Fat 275); Fat 31g (Saturated 11g); Cholesterol 116mg; Sodium 470mg; Carbohydrate 8g (Dietary Fiber 1g); Protein 33g.

Caraway Pork Roast with Sauerkraut

Pork and sauerkraut are a classic German food combination. The addition of caraway seeds adds a delicious nutty flavor to the pork as it cooks. I find that a center cut of meat comes out the best in this recipe.

Preparation time: *20 minutes*

Cooking time: *30 minutes under pressure*

Pressure level: *High*

Yield: *6 servings*

4 cloves garlic, minced

1½ teaspoons caraway seeds

1 teaspoon salt

¼ teaspoon pepper

2½ to 3-pound boneless pork loin roast

1 tablespoon olive oil

1 large onion, thinly sliced

1 can (12 ounces) beer

1 pound sauerkraut, drained and rinsed under cold water

1 bay leaf

½ cup chicken broth

1 Combine the garlic, caraway seeds, salt, and pepper in a small bowl to form a paste. With a knife, score the top and bottom of the roast, all over, about ⅛ inch deep. Rub the garlic mixture into the cuts.

2 Heat the olive oil in a pressure cooker over high heat. Add the roast and brown evenly on all sides. Remove the roast.

3 Add the onion and cook for 1 minute. Add the beer. Cook for 1 minute. Add the sauerkraut, bay leaf, and chicken broth. Place the roast on top of the sauerkraut.

4 Cover and bring to high pressure over high heat. Lower the heat to stabilize the pressure. Cook for 35 minutes.

5 Remove from the heat. Release the pressure with a quick-release method. Unlock and remove the cover. Test the roast with a fork; the fork should penetrate easily. If not tender, cover and cook under pressure for an additional 10 minutes.

6 Remove the roast and let sit for 10 minutes before slicing.

Per serving: Calories 395 (From Fat 203); Fat 23g (Saturated 8g); Cholesterol 115mg; Sodium 832mg; Carbohydrate 6g (Dietary Fiber 3g); Protein 40g.

New England Boiled Dinner

This was one of the first dishes I ever made in a pressure cooker. Although this recipe is very similar to corned beef and cabbage, a smoked pork butt gives delicious results in less time than corned beef. Available in your supermarket meat case, smoked pork butts are traditionally wrapped in red plastic. Remove any netting or coverings before cooking.

Preparation time: *15 minutes*

Cooking time: *24 minutes under pressure*

Pressure level: *High*

Yield: *4 to 6 servings*

2 cups water

1 bay leaf

4 cloves garlic, crushed

½ teaspoon whole black peppercorns

2-pound smoked pork butt

1 pound small red or new potatoes, cut in half

2 large carrots, peeled and cut into 1-inch pieces

2 leeks, or 8 scallions, cleaned well and cut into 1-inch pieces

1 small head green cabbage, cored and quartered

1 Add the water, bay leaf, garlic, and peppercorns to a pressure cooker. Place a steaming basket in the pressure cooker. Place the pork butt in the basket.

2 Cover and bring to high pressure over high heat. Lower the heat to stabilize the pressure. Cook for 20 minutes.

3 Remove from the heat. Release the pressure with a quick-release method. Unlock and remove the cover. Add the potatoes, carrots, leeks, and cabbage. Reposition the cover and bring to high pressure over high heat. Lower the heat to stabilize the pressure. Cook for 4 minutes.

4 Remove from the heat. Release the pressure with a quick-release method. Unlock and remove the cover.

5 Remove the vegetables with a slotted spoon to a large serving platter. Slice the pork as thin as possible. Spoon some of the cooking liquid over the meat and vegetables.

Per serving: Calories 447 (From Fat 241); Fat 27g (Saturated 9g); Cholesterol 86mg; Sodium 1,815mg; Carbohydrate 27g (Dietary Fiber 7g); Protein 24g.

Moroccan Chicken

Simplicity at its best! You don't even have to brown the chicken. Just heat the olive oil and add the remaining ingredients. The resulting flavor and aroma is, well, amazing! If you want to cut some calories, you can even remove the chicken skin.

Preparation time: *10 minutes*

Cooking time: *15 minutes under pressure*

Pressure level: *High*

Yield: *4 servings*

4 tablespoons olive oil	*4 threads saffron (optional)*
1 large onion, sliced	*One 3- to 4-pound chicken, quartered*
1 clove garlic, thinly sliced	*1 cup chicken broth*
2 tablespoons minced flat-leaf parsley	*1 large lemon, thinly sliced*
1 tablespoon minced cilantro	*8 large green Sicilian olives*
1 teaspoon salt	*1 package (10 ounces) couscous (see Chapter 8 for more information about couscous)*
½ teaspoon black pepper	

1 Heat the olive oil in a pressure cooker over medium-high heat. Add the onion, garlic, 1 tablespoon of the parsley, cilantro, salt, pepper, and, if desired, the saffron. Stir well. Add the chicken. Stir to coat with the onion mixture. Pour the broth over the chicken; do not stir. Place the lemon slices on top of the chicken.

2 Cover and bring to high pressure over high heat. Lower the heat to stabilize the pressure. Cook for 15 minutes.

3 Remove from the heat. Let the pressure drop using a quick-release method.

4 Unlock and remove the cover.

5 Remove the chicken with a slotted spoon to a platter. Cover to keep warm.

6 Reduce the cooking liquid over high heat until the sauce is thick. Add the olives and cook until warmed through. Pour the sauce over the chicken. Sprinkle with the remaining 1 tablespoon parsley.

7 Serve with cooked couscous, prepared according to package directions.

Per serving: *Calories 791 (From Fat 335); Fat 37g (Saturated 8g); Cholesterol 167mg; Sodium 1,142mg; Carbohydrate 59g (Dietary Fiber 5g); Protein 52g.*

Chicken Cacciatore

Cacciatore means "hunter's style" and refers to how Italian hunters used to prepare small game out in the open. Today, cacciatore dishes are usually made with cut-up chicken pieces. I like to serve this dish (pictured on the front cover) with white rice to absorb the delicious sauce.

Preparation time: *20 minutes*

Cooking time: *10 minutes under pressure*

Pressure level: *High*

Yield: *4 servings*

2 tablespoons olive oil

4-pound chicken, skin and excess fat removed, cut into serving pieces (see Figure 7-3)

1 large onion, chopped

2 cloves garlic, peeled and very thinly sliced

1 small pickled cherry or jalapeño pepper, seeded and coarsely chopped (optional)

8 ounces white mushrooms, thinly sliced

⅓ cup dry white wine

1 can (28 ounces) crushed tomatoes

1 teaspoon salt

¼ teaspoon black pepper

1 tablespoon minced parsley

2 cups cooked white rice

1 Heat the olive oil in a pressure cooker over medium-high heat. Brown the chicken pieces in batches and set them aside on a large plate. Add the onion, garlic, cherry pepper (if desired), and mushrooms. Cook for 2 minutes. Return the browned chicken to the pressure cooker. Add the wine, tomatoes, salt, and black pepper. Cook for 2 minutes.

2 Cover and bring to high pressure over high heat. Lower the heat to stabilize the pressure. Cook for 10 minutes.

3 Remove from the heat. Release the pressure with a quick-release method. Unlock and remove the cover.

4 Transfer to a serving dish and garnish with the parsley. Serve with the white rice.

Per serving: *Calories 470 (From Fat 174); Fat 19g (Saturated 4g); Cholesterol 93mg; Sodium 1,280mg; Carbohydrate 38g (Dietary Fiber 3g); Protein 34g.*

Braised Turkey Breast

I came across this recipe a few years ago. I used to make it in a large Dutch oven, letting the turkey simmer for 2 hours. One day it dawned on me that I could get the job done in less than half the time in a pressure cooker. This is now the only way I'll cook turkey breast!

Preparation time: *15 minutes*

Cooking time: *40 minutes under pressure*

Pressure level: *High*

Yield: *6 servings*

Salt and pepper

4- to 5-pound whole turkey breast, wings removed, rinsed under cold water and patted dry

2 tablespoons vegetable oil

1 onion, thinly sliced

2 garlic cloves, crushed

2 carrots, peeled and thinly sliced

2 stalks celery, thinly sliced

1 cup chicken broth

1 cup dry red wine

1 tablespoon cornstarch

2 tablespoons water

1 Generously salt and pepper the turkey breast.

2 Heat the oil in a pressure cooker over medium-high heat. Add the turkey breast and brown on all sides. Remove and set aside. Add the onion, garlic, carrots, and celery. Cook until the onion is soft. Add the broth and wine. Cook for 2 minutes. Place the turkey breast in the pressure cooker.

3 Cover and bring to high pressure over high heat. Lower the heat to stabilize the pressure. Cook for 40 minutes.

4 Remove from the heat. Release the pressure with a quick-release method.

5 Unlock and remove the cover. Carefully remove the turkey and place on a large plate. Cover with foil.

6 Strain the cooking liquid. Pour it back into the pressure cooker and boil it down by a third. Combine the cornstarch and water. Add to the cooking liquid and whisk until thickened. Season to taste with salt and pepper.

7 Slice the turkey off the carcass, as shown in Figure 7-4. Serve with the gravy.

Per serving: Calories 433 (From Fat 180); Fat 20g (Saturated 5g); Cholesterol 149mg; Sodium 390mg; Carbohydrate 1g (Dietary Fiber 0g); Protein 58g.

Cutting Up a Raw Chicken

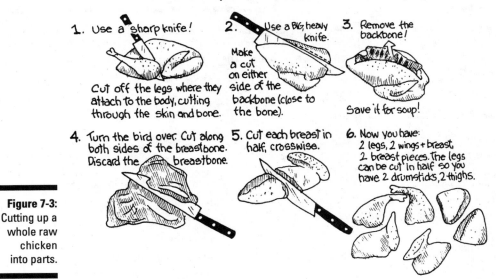

1. Use a sharp knife! Cut off the legs where they attach to the body, cutting through the skin and bone.

2. Use a BIG, heavy knife. Make a cut on either side of the backbone (close to the bone).

3. Remove the backbone! Save it for soup!

4. Turn the bird over. Cut along both sides of the breastbone. Discard the breastbone.

5. Cut each breast in half, crosswise.

6. Now you have: 2 legs, 2 wings + breast, 2 breast pieces. The legs can be cut in half so you have 2 drumsticks, 2 thighs.

Figure 7-3:
Cutting up a whole raw chicken into parts.

CARVING A TURKEY BREAST

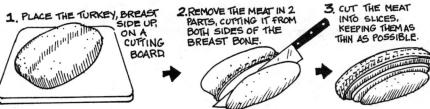

1. PLACE THE TURKEY, BREAST SIDE UP, ON A CUTTING BOARD.

2. REMOVE THE MEAT IN 2 PARTS, CUTTING IT FROM BOTH SIDES OF THE BREAST BONE.

3. CUT THE MEAT INTO SLICES, KEEPING THEM AS THIN AS POSSIBLE.

Figure 7-4:
Carving a turkey breast is easy.

Chapter 8

Fork-Tender Stews

Stews are an economical way of stretching a pound or two of inexpensive cuts of meat or poultry — along with garden-fresh veggies, herbs, and spices — into dinner for eight. Because the objective is to have a melding of flavors, choose ingredients that complement each other as their flavors come together while cooking.

Although stews are usually considered a slow-simmered food, you'll be amazed by how you can get the same results in the pressure cooker in less than half the time — without sacrificing flavor or appearance. The trick is coaxing the optimum flavor from each ingredient.

Flavor, Flavor, Flavor: The Makings of a Great Stew!

Nothing is worse than a watery, tasteless stew, especially when it's so easy to make when done right! Making stew is like building a house. First, you have to build the foundation by choosing the main ingredient, be it meat, poultry, or even root vegetables. Then you need the structure to bring it all together — perhaps a flavorful broth, some vegetable purée, or hearty wine or malt-flavored beer? Next, you need to add some decorative yet essential touches in the form of vibrant, colored, flavorful vegetables such as carrots, peas, string beans, or perhaps some starchy potatoes for added body. Finally, you can spark things up with a sprinkling of herbs and spices, both dried and fresh. By the time you're done, you'll have the tastiest, best-smelling stew around!

A cut above the rest

Choosing the right cut of meat is as important when making a stew as it is when making a braised roast. And the more expensive cuts aren't necessarily the best!

I always avoid purchasing prepackaged stew meat. I find that what appears on the top of the package is not always representative of what's on the bottom. Resourceful supermarkets have been known to conceal gristle and fatty pieces under better ones. For best results, do like I do and purchase a nice top round London broil or roast. Remove all the visible fat and cut the meat into uniform-sized pieces. You can do the same thing with pork and lamb. A nice center cut piece of pork loin or a small boneless leg of lamb turns into great stew meat.

If you want to use chicken, boneless chicken thighs make a great stew as long as you remove the excess fat. Boneless white breast meat can be dry, and the flavor can cook out. To prevent this from happening, use breast meat only in recipes that have an intense, powerful flavor.

Browning your meat

Browning the meat or poultry is one of the first steps when preparing stews in a pressure cooker. Browning in hot oil seals in the natural juices and caramelizes the exterior so that the meat or poultry looks and tastes better. For best results, follow these suggestions:

✔ Always make sure that the oil is very hot before adding the meat or poultry.

✔ Dry the meat or poultry by patting it with paper towels before browning. This step prevents the hot oil from dropping dramatically in temperature when the raw food is added.

✔ Brown in batches. If you put too much raw meat or poultry into the hot oil, the oil has a hard time coming back up to the correct temperature. The food will sputter rather than sizzle as it steams, releasing its natural juices rather than browning and sealing them in.

Sautéing and deglazing

Sautéed onions, garlic, gingerroot (see Figure 8-1), and peppers add tremendous flavor to a stew. These ingredients need to be cooked until soft and perhaps a bit browned.

Don't cook with what you wouldn't drink!

Purchasing wine to drink can be, at best, intimidating for the uninitiated. Buying wine for cooking can also cause some anxiety. A good rule to follow is, if you wouldn't drink it, don't cook with it! If you're uncertain about what wine to purchase, go a local, reputable liquor store and ask for some advice. Never use cooking wine that is marketed as such and sold in grocery stores. These wines are loaded with sodium and are of poor quality that can mask the fresh flavor of your ingredients.

Cook onions, garlic, gingerroot and peppers only to the golden brown stage — never deeper — or they'll make the stew bitter.

Figure 8-1:
Fresh
gingerroot.

Once they food is done browning, you need to deglaze the pan, as shown in Figure 8-2. *Deglazing* means loosening up and dissolving all of the caramelized juices from browning the meat, poultry, or other ingredients. You do so by adding liquid such as chopped or puréed tomatoes, wine, beer, broth, or even water. You bring this liquid to a boil and quickly stir and scrape the bottom of the pot with a large kitchen spoon. The aroma will be heavenly!

DEGLAZING A PAN.....

1. ONCE YOU ARE DONE BROWNING, YOU NEED TO DEGLAZE THE PAN. (YOU WANT TO LOOSEN UP/DISSOLVE ALL OF THE CARAMELIZED JUICES FROM BROWNING MEAT, POULTRY, ONIONS, ETC...

☆ REMOVE THE BROWNED ITEM FROM THE PAN.

2. DO SO, BY ADDING LIQUID (CHOPPED OR PUREED TOMATOES, WINE, BEER, BROTH OR WATER).

RAISE HEAT AND QUICKLY BRING TO A BOIL.

3. QUICKLY... STIR AND SCRAPE THE BOTTOM OF THE POT WITH A LARGE KITCHEN SPOON. BOIL UNTIL THE SAUCE... ...IS REDUCED BY HALF

THE AROMA SHOULD BE HEAVENLY

SPOON OVER COOKED MEAT, POULTRY OR FISH !

Figure 8-2:
Steps for
deglazing
a pan.

Season away!

Well-seasoned food makes for delectable, delicious food. By just having a few herbs (see Figure 8-3) and spices on hand, you'll be amazed how easy it is to transform plain food into a culinary masterpiece!

- **Salt and black pepper:** I like to usually generously salt and pepper the meat and poultry after I pat it dry, right before browning it in the hot oil. Doing so seems to intensify the flavor immensely.

  I always use kosher salt. Because it doesn't contain any of the additives found in table salt, it tastes better. Table salt contains free-flowing agents, so it doesn't stick to food as well as kosher salt.

  If you don't have a pepper mill already, do yourself a favor and pick one up. Nothing beats the flavor of freshly ground black pepper. Preground pepper lacks all of the intensity of the freshly ground stuff and should be banned from cooking!

  If you season the meat or poultry before browning, you probably won't have to add any additional salt and pepper. As with all recipes, however, always taste the food before serving to make sure that it's well seasoned.

- **Bay leaf:** A member of the evergreen family, this aromatic herb imparts wonderful flavor to almost everything. Fresh bay leaves aren't always readily available, but dried leaves are. A leaf or two is usually all you need.

- **Dried thyme:** This is one of my favorite herbs to use in cooking. A bit more subtle than oregano, with tones of mint, thyme provides a well-rounded flavor to most dishes when used judiciously.

- **Sage:** With a pungent, almost musty taste and aroma, sage goes well with most poultry and pork. Fresh sage leaves can be found in the produce section of most supermarkets.

- **Fresh parsley:** I like to finish some stews with a healthy sprinkling of minced parsley. If added at the beginning of the recipe, the parsley loses its flavor and bright green color. Therefore, always add it right before serving. Never use curly parsley. I prefer the Italian, or flat-leaf, variety, which is easier to mince and is more flavorful.

Figure 8-3:
Herbs can make your stews even more flavorful.

The veggies

Although tough cuts of meat cook up fork-tender in the pressure cooker, they do need to cook longer than most vegetables. You will, therefore, cook the meat under pressure until almost ready before adding the vegetables 4 to 8 minutes before the stew is done cooking. For example, look at My Favorite Beef Stew recipe in this chapter. You first cook the meat for 15 minutes under pressure. After releasing the pressure, you add all the vegetables except the mushrooms, and cook them under pressure for 8 minutes. Release the pressure again, add the mushrooms, and cook them for 1 minute. Our rich-tasting, delicious stew is ready from start to finish in less than 45 minutes! (See Chapter 3 for more information on stop-and-go cooking.)

When Is It Going to Be Done?

Although later in this chapter I share with you some of my favorite stew recipes and their respective cooking times, I also give you some basic pressure-cooker cooking times for commonly used stew meats and poultry pieces in Table 8-1. That way, you can adapt your favorite traditional stew recipes so you can make them in your pressure cooker.

All cooking times are at best approximations and should be used as a general guideline. The cooking times in Table 8-1 begin when the pressure cooker reaches high pressure. Always start with the shortest cooking time; you can always continue cooking under pressure for an additional couple minutes until the desired texture is reached. Not all cuts of meat cook for the same amount of time. You may also find that your particular brand or model of pressure cooker cooks faster or even a bit slower. Therefore, feel free to note any cooking time differences in the right-hand column of the table.

Table 8-1	Recommended Pressure-Cooker Cooking Times for Meat and Poultry	
Food	*Cooking Time (in Minutes)*	*Your Notes*
Beef, pork or lamb, 1- to 2-inch cubes	15 to 20	
Meatballs, browned	8 to 10	
Chicken, boneless breast or thighs, 1-inch pieces	8 to 10	
Chicken, pieces	10 to 12	

Stews: Meals of Convenience

For me, stew is synonymous with convenience. A combination of meat or poultry, vegetables, and other ingredients brought together in a flavorful sauce or gravy, these one-pot meals are usually quick and easy to make, especially in the pressure cooker. I've assembled a few of my favorite recipes to share with you, including one for a vegetarian version of the zesty Moroccan stew called *tagine*.

Tagine is meant to be eaten with couscous. Over the past ten to twenty years, as ethnic dining has expanded beyond take-out Chinese and pizza, Americans have been exposed to many new and exotic foods and ingredients used in other parts of the world. Ingredients such as cilantro and tofu have become as common in our pantries and fridges as spaghetti and ketchup. Couscous is one of these foods, formerly unheard of — now commonplace.

A staple of North Africa, couscous is a type of pasta made with semolina flour. When making couscous in the traditional manner, Arabic women mix the semolina with a small amount of water to make a paste. They then rub the paste through a fine mesh screen. The resulting dried pellets are sun-dried and stored for later use. Fortunately for us, commercially made couscous can be purchased at most supermarkets, usually in the aisle with the rice and noodle mixes.

My Favorite Beef Stew

I'm of Italian descent, so I believe that beef stew should be red with tomatoes and red wine. It also needs to be full of great vegetables and served over egg noodles.

Preparation time: *20 minutes*

Cooking time: *24 minutes under pressure*

Pressure level: *High*

Yield: *6 servings*

Salt and pepper

½ pounds top round or chuck, trimmed of all fat, cut into 1-inch cubes

3 tablespoons olive oil

1 large onion, chopped

3 cloves garlic, minced

¾ cup red wine

1 can (14½ ounces) diced tomatoes

½ teaspoon dried thyme

1 bay leaf

8 ounces green beans, ends trimmed and cut into 1-inch pieces

8 ounces baby carrots

2 stalks celery, cut into 1-inch pieces

1 large potato, peeled and cut into 1-inch chunks

8 ounces white button mushrooms, quartered

2 tablespoons flat-leaf Italian parsley, minced

8 ounces cooked broad noodles for serving

1 Generously salt and pepper the meat. Heat 2 tablespoons of the olive oil in a pressure cooker over high heat. Brown the meat in two batches. Remove and set aside in a large bowl. Add the remaining 1 tablespoon of olive oil. Add the onion and garlic. Cook until the onion is soft. Return the browned meat to the pressure cooker. Add the wine. Bring to a boil and cook for 2 minutes. Add the tomatoes, dried thyme, and bay leaf.

2 Cover and bring to high pressure over high heat. Lower the heat to stabilize the pressure. Cook for 15 minutes.

3 Remove from the heat. Let the pressure drop using a quick-release method. Unlock and remove the cover.

4 Add the green beans, carrots, celery, and potatoes.

5 Cover and bring to high pressure over high heat. Lower the heat to stabilize the pressure. Cook for 8 minutes.

6 Remove from the heat. Let the pressure drop using a quick-release method. Unlock and remove the cover.

7 Season to taste with salt and pepper. Add the mushrooms.

8 Cover and bring to high pressure over high heat. Lower the heat to stabilize the pressure. Cook for 1 minute.

9 Remove from the heat. Let the pressure drop using a quick-release method.

10 Unlock and remove the cover. Stir in the parsley before serving. Serve with the noodles.

Per serving: Calories 426 (From Fat 115); Fat 13g (Saturated 3g); Cholesterol 101mg; Sodium 277mg; Carbohydrate 44g (Dietary Fiber 6g); Protein 34g.

Meatball Stew

When I was growing up, my mother used to make a meatball stew very similar to this one. You can substitute prepared frozen meatballs from the supermarket. The cooking time under pressure won't be affected, only the time it takes to reach it.

Preparation time: *20 minutes*

Cooking time: *10 minutes under pressure*

Pressure level: *High*

Yield: *4 servings*

1 pound lean ground beef	*1 medium onion, chopped*
2 large eggs	*4 cloves garlic, minced*
½ cup plain bread crumbs	*1 package (10 ounces) frozen peas and carrots*
4 tablespoons minced flat-leaf Italian parsley	*2 large potatoes, peeled and cut into 2-inch chunks*
4 tablespoons grated pecorino Romano cheese	*1 can (29 ounces) tomato sauce*
1 teaspoon salt	*1 teaspoon dried Italian seasoning*
⅛ teaspoon pepper	*Salt and pepper to taste*
3 tablespoons olive oil	

1 Combine the ground beef, eggs, bread crumbs, 2 tablespoons of the parsley, cheese, salt, and pepper in a large mixing bowl. Do not overmix. Shape into 8 meatballs.

2 Heat the olive oil in a pressure cooker over high heat. Brown the meatballs. Remove the meatballs and pour out all but 1 tablespoon of the cooking oil. Add the onion and garlic. Cook over medium-high heat until the onion is soft. Add the peas and carrots, potatoes, tomato sauce, and Italian seasoning. Drop in the meatballs, one at a time.

3 Cover and bring to high pressure over high heat. Lower the heat to stabilize the pressure. Cook for 10 minutes.

4 Remove from the heat. Let the pressure drop using a quick-release method.

5 Unlock and remove the cover. Season with salt and pepper. Stir in the remaining 2 tablespoons parsley before serving.

Per serving: Calories 604 (From Fat 251); Fat 28g (Saturated 8g); Cholesterol 118mg; Sodium 2,319mg; Carbohydrate 56g (Dietary Fiber 8g); Protein 36g.

Irish Lamb Stew

A peasant dish made with readily available ingredients, authentic Irish lamb stew is simplicity at its best. A true meat and potato dish, you can also add 3 large carrots, cut lengthwise and then into 1-inch pieces, along with the potatoes.

Preparation time: *20 minutes*

Cooking time: *28 minutes under pressure*

Pressure level: *High*

Yield: *8 servings*

Salt and pepper

2 pounds boneless lamb shoulder, trimmed of all fat and cut into 2-inch cubes

3 tablespoons olive oil

2 large onions, chopped

1¼ cups water

2 pounds all-purpose potatoes, peeled and cut into 2-inch chunks

3 tablespoons flat-leaf Italian parsley, minced

1 Generously salt and pepper the lamb.

2 Heat 2 tablespoons of the olive oil in a pressure cooker over high heat. Brown the meat in three batches. Remove and set aside in a large bowl. Add the remaining 1 tablespoon olive oil. Add the onions and cook until soft. Return the browned meat with any accumulated juices to the pressure cooker. Add the water and 1 teaspoon salt.

3 Cover and bring to high pressure over high heat. Lower the heat to stabilize the pressure. Cook for 20 minutes.

4 Remove from the heat. Let the pressure drop using a quick-release method.

5 Unlock and remove the cover.

6 Add the potatoes.

7 Cover and bring to high pressure over high heat. Lower the heat to stabilize the pressure. Cook for 8 minutes.

8 Remove from the heat. Let the pressure drop using a quick-release method.

9 Unlock and remove the cover.

10 If the stew is very liquidy, bring it to a boil, uncovered, and cook until the sauce thickens. Season to taste with salt and pepper. Stir in the parsley before serving.

Per serving: *Calories 395 (From Fat 161); Fat 18g (Saturated 5g); Cholesterol 147mg; Sodium 108mg; Carbohydrate 23g (Dietary Fiber 3g); Protein 34g.*

Pork and Mustard Stew

What a wonderfully flavored stew, perfect for a fall or winter meal. The addition of whole-seed mustard right before serving gives this stew an added taste punch.

Preparation time: *20 minutes*

Cooking time: *14 minutes*

Pressure level: *High*

Yield: *6 to 8 servings*

Salt and pepper

2 pounds lean pork loin, cut into 1-inch cubes

2 tablespoons olive oil

2 large onions, chopped

2 cloves garlic, chopped

1 tablespoon all-purpose flour

¾ cup dry red wine

¾ cup beef or chicken broth

5 fresh sage leaves, chopped

8 small red or new potatoes, scrubbed, peeled, and quartered

1 large carrot, thinly sliced

1½ tablespoons whole-seed mustard

2 tablespoons minced flat-leaf Italian parsley

1 Generously salt and pepper the pork loin. Set aside.

2 Heat the olive oil in a pressure cooker over medium-high heat. Add the onions and garlic. Cook until the onion is soft. Raise the heat to high. Add the pork and cook until golden. Sprinkle with the flour. Stir well. Add the wine, broth, and sage.

3 Cover and bring to high pressure over high heat. Lower the heat to stabilize the pressure. Cook for 10 minutes.

4 Remove from the heat. Let the pressure drop using a quick-release method.

5 Unlock and remove the cover.

6 Add the potatoes and carrots.

7 Cover and bring to high pressure over high heat. Lower the heat to stabilize the pressure. Cook for 8 minutes.

8 Remove from the heat. Let the pressure drop using a quick-release method.

9 Unlock and remove the cover.

10 Season to taste with salt and pepper. Stir in the mustard and parsley before serving.

Per serving: Calories 279 (From Fat 108); Fat 12g (Saturated 3g); Cholesterol 68mg; Sodium 218mg; Carbohydrate 14g (Dietary Fiber 2g); Protein 28g.

Pork Stew with Green Beans and Mushrooms

I don't know whether it's the combination of meat, green beans, and mushrooms in a light, flavorful sauce, but this stew is special enough to be served to company with parsleyed potatoes or buttered noodles.

Preparation time: *20 minutes*

Cooking time: *14 minutes under pressure*

Pressure level: *High*

Yield: *6 to 8 servings*

Salt and pepper

2 pounds lean pork loin, cut into 1-inch cubes

2 tablespoons olive oil

1 large onion, chopped

2 cloves garlic, peeled and chopped

2 tablespoons all-purpose flour

¾ cup beer or dry white wine

¾ cup chicken broth

½ teaspoon dried thyme

2 packages (10 ounces each) frozen French-cut green beans

¾ pound fresh white button mushrooms, quartered

2 tablespoons minced flat-leaf Italian parsley

1 Generously salt and pepper the pork loin. Set aside.

2 Heat the olive oil in the pressure cooker over medium-high heat. Add the onion and garlic. Cook until the onion is soft. Raise the heat to high. Add the pork loin and cook for 6 minutes. Sprinkle with the flour. Stir well. Add the beer, broth, and thyme.

3 Cover and bring to high pressure over high heat. Lower the heat to stabilize the pressure. Cook for 10 minutes.

4 Remove from the heat. Let the pressure drop using a quick-release method.

5 Unlock and remove the cover.

6 Add the green beans and mushrooms.

7 Cover and bring to high pressure over high heat. Lower the heat to stabilize the pressure. Cook for 4 minutes.

8 Remove from the heat. Let the pressure drop using a quick-release method.

9 Unlock and remove the cover. Taste and adjust for salt and black pepper. If too much liquid, bring to a boil and reduce until the sauce is thick. Stir in the parsley before serving.

Per serving: *Calories 226 (From Fat 77); Fat 9g (Saturated 3g); Cholesterol 69mg; Sodium 215mg; Carbohydrate 10g (Dietary Fiber 3g); Protein 27g.*

Indian Butter Chicken

When I was invited to teach cooking classes at a few shopping malls in Pennsylvania, I needed a recipe that was simple to prepare and large enough to feed a crowd. It also had to be big on flavor and aroma. I found just what I was looking for when I came across a recipe for Indian Butter Chicken in a magazine. After making a few changes here and there, I was able to adapt this great dish so that it can be made in the pressure cooker.

Preparation time: *15 minutes*

Cooking time: *8 minutes under pressure*

Pressure level: *High*

Yield: *6 servings*

1 tablespoon vegetable oil	*2 teaspoons garam masala spice blend (see the Tip at the end of this recipe)*
Salt and pepper	
1½ pounds boneless chicken breast cut into ¾-inch cubes	*1 can (6 ounces) tomato paste*
	2 cups chicken broth
2 tablespoons vegetable oil	*½ cup heavy cream*
1 large onion, minced	*2 tablespoons minced cilantro*
1 tablespoon minced or grated gingerroot	*3 tablespoons butter, cut into small pieces*
1 small jalapeño, seeded and minced	*1 lime, cut into 6 pieces*

1 Generously salt and pepper the chicken. Heat the vegetable oil in a pressure cooker over high heat. Add the onion, gingerroot, and jalapeño. Cook for 3 minutes. Add the chicken and cook until no longer pink on the outside (chicken will still be raw on the inside). Add the tomato paste and chicken broth. Stir well.

2 Cover and bring to high pressure over high heat. Lower the heat to stabilize the pressure. Cook for 8 minutes.

3 Remove from the heat. Let the pressure drop using a quick-release method.

4 Unlock and remove the cover.

5 Over low heat, stir in the heavy cream. Add the cilantro and butter. Stir until the butter melts. Serve with white rice or Yellow Split Pea and Basmati Pilaf in Chapter 5.

6 Squeeze juice from the lime wedges over the servings.

Tip: *Garam masala spice blend is readily available at most Indian and specialty food stores. You can make your own by combining ¾ teaspoon ground cumin, ½ teaspoon paprika, ¼ teaspoon ground cinnamon, ⅛ teaspoon ground cayenne, ⅛ teaspoon ground cloves, and 1 bay leaf, crumbled, in a small bowl. Store in an airtight jar.*

Per serving: *Calories 448 (From Fat 297); Fat 33g (Saturated 15g); Cholesterol 137mg; Sodium 520mg; Carbohydrate 11g (Dietary Fiber 2g); Protein 27g.*

Sweet-and-Sour Chicken

Sweet-and-Sour Chicken is a Chinese-restaurant favorite among baby boomers. This pressure cooker adaptation is one of the easiest and quickest recipes I know for getting dinner on the table in 30 minutes or less from start to finish.

Preparation time: *15 minutes*

Cooking time: *10 minutes under pressure*

Pressure level: *High*

Yield: *4 to 6 servings*

1 tablespoon vegetable oil

1 large onion, chopped

1 large green bell pepper, cored, seeded, and diced

1 large red bell pepper, cored, seeded, and diced

2 pounds boneless chicken thighs, trimmed of all visible fat, cut into 1-inch pieces

2 tablespoons soy sauce

1½ cups prepared sweet-and-sour or duck sauce

1 tablespoon apple-cider vinegar

3 tablespoons water

1 teaspoon garlic powder

2 scallions, white and green parts, thinly sliced

2 cups cooked white rice

1 Heat the oil in a pressure cooker over medium-high heat. Add the onion and the red and green bell peppers. Cook for 2 minutes. Add the chicken and soy sauce. Cook for 3 minutes. Add the sweet-and-sour sauce, vinegar, water, and garlic powder. Stir well.

2 Cover and bring to high pressure. Lower the heat to stabilize the pressure. Cook for 10 minutes.

3 Remove from the heat. Let the pressure drop using a quick-release method.

4 Unlock and remove the cover.

5 Transfer to a serving dish and garnish with the scallions. Serve with the rice.

Per serving: *Calories 385 (From Fat 136); Fat 15g (Saturated 4g); Cholesterol 71mg; Sodium 788mg; Carbohydrate 40g (Dietary Fiber 2g); Protein 22g.*

☞ Vegetable Tagine with Couscous

Tagine, pronounced "ta-JEAN," is a type of thick Moroccan stew. Usually made with meats like lamb and goat, or chicken, tagines also can be made with all vegetables, such as this recipe. Serve it with couscous.

Preparation time: *10 minutes*

Cooking time: *35 minutes under pressure*

Pressure level: *High*

Yield: *4 to 6 servings*

2 tablespoons olive oil

1 large red onion, coarsely chopped

2 cloves garlic, crushed

1½ teaspoons ground cumin

1 teaspoon paprika

½ teaspoon ground cinnamon

2 teaspoons salt

¼ teaspoon black pepper

1 can (14½ ounces) diced tomatoes

1 red bell pepper, cored, seeded, and diced

1 green bell pepper, cored, seeded, and diced

2 carrots, peeled and cut into ½-inch pieces

2 stalks celery, cut into ½-inch pieces

2 cups peeled, cubed butternut squash

1 cup cooked chickpeas

8 ounces green beans, trimmed and cut into 1-inch pieces

1½ cups vegetable or chicken stock or broth

Salt to taste

2 tablespoons minced flat-leaf Italian parsley

1 package (10 ounces) couscous (see the sidebar on couscous in this chapter)

1 Heat the olive oil in a pressure cooker over medium-high heat. Add the onion and garlic. Cook until the onion is soft. Add the cumin, paprika, cinnamon, salt, and black pepper. Cook for 2 minutes. Add the tomatoes and red and green peppers. Cook for 2 minutes. Add the carrots, celery, squash, chickpeas, green beans, and stock.

2 Cover and bring to high pressure over high heat. Lower the heat to stabilize the pressure. Cook for 5 minutes.

3 Remove from the heat. Let the pressure drop using a quick-release method.

4 Unlock and remove the cover.

5 Taste the vegetables. If they're still hard, return to Step 2 and cook them for an additional 1 to 3 minutes, or until tender.

6 Season with salt. Add the parsley. Serve with the couscous, prepared according to package instructions.

Per serving: *Calories 355 (From Fat 56); Fat 6g (Saturated 1g); Cholesterol 0mg; Sodium 1,252mg; Carbohydrate 66g (Dietary Fiber 11g); Protein 12g.*

Part IV

Complements to the Meal: Side Dishes, Condiments, and Sweet Endings

The 5th Wave   By Rich Tennant

AFTER PRESSURE COOKING THEIR DINNER, THE HINKLEYS ENGAGE IN PRESSURE EATING TO THE MUSIC OF KHATCHATURIAN'S "THE SABRE DANCE."

In this part...

Sometimes I wish I could just skip dinner and head straight for the dessert, especially when it's one of the delicious cheesecakes, custards, or puddings from this part of the book. Since many people like to give gifts from the kitchen, I'm also going to share with you a few of my quick and easy recipes for fruit jams and a chutney too, perfect for holiday gift giving.

Chapter 9

Vegetables: Nature's Bounty

• •

In This Chapter

▶ Using the pressure cooker to save time and nutrients

▶ Making fresh, delicious vegetable side dishes and salads

• •

I've never met a vegetable I didn't like. Each one has its own unique characteristics and taste. Unfortunately, too many people have this thing against these green, yellow, orange, and red foods. Vegetables are full of vitamins and minerals and, when cooked properly, are quite tasty, too! Even a supermarket rotisserie chicken warrants a veggie side dish or two, and this is where your pressure cooker comes in. Why make powdery instant potatoes when in about the same amount of time you can have the real thing, all hot and steaming with a pat of melting butter dripping down the sides? Fresh vegetables and the pressure cooker were made for each other, especially when you're short on time.

Saving Time and Nutrients

Cooking vegetables in a pressure cooker cuts back on the cooking time by up to 70 percent. But besides saving you time, vegetables cooked under pressure can also be more nutritious for you. When cooked or steamed in a conventional pot, some of the water-soluble nutrients get washed away. When the vegetables are cooked in a pressure cooker, however, they cook so quickly that they maintain more nutrients and keep their natural, vibrant colors and flavors.

To facilitate things for you, I've compiled Table 9-1, which gives approximate cooking times for vegetables. The cooking times begin when the pressure cooker reaches high pressure. Remember that most vegetables cook very quickly; if cooked 30 to 60 seconds too long, your crisp broccoli becomes mush! Always err on the side of being underdone. Start with the shortest cooking time; you can always continue cooking under pressure for an additional couple of minutes until the desired texture is reached.

All cooking times are approximations and should be used as general guidelines. Not all types of red potatoes cook for the same amount of time, for example. You may also find that your particular brand or model of pressure cooker cooks faster or even a bit slower. Therefore, feel free to note any cooking time differences in the right-hand column of Table 9-1.

Table 9-1	Recommended Pressure Cooker Cooking Times for Vegetables	
Food	*Cooking Time (in Minutes)*	*Your Notes*
Artichokes, hearts	2 to 3	
Artichokes, whole	8 to 10	
Asparagus	1 to 2	
Beans, fresh green or wax, whole or pieces	2 to 3	
Beans, lima, shelled	2 to 3	
Beets, ¼-inch slices	3 to 4	
Beets, whole, peeled	12 to 14	
Broccoli, florets or spear	2 to 3	
Brussels sprouts, whole	3 to 4	
Cabbage, red or green, quartered	3 to 4	
Carrots, ¼-inch slices	1 to 2	
Carrots, whole baby	2 to 3	
Cauliflower, florets	2 to 3	
Collard greens	4 to 5	
Corn on the cob	3 to 4	
Escarole	1 to 2	
Okra	2 to 3	

Food	Cooking Time (in Minutes)	Your Notes
Parsnips, 1-inch pieces	2 to 3	
Peas, shelled	1 to 1½	
Potatoes, pieces or sliced	5 to 7	
Potatoes, whole, small or new	5 to 7	
Potatoes, whole, medium	10 to 12	
Pumpkin, peeled, 1-inch chunks	2 to 3	
Rutabaga, 1-inch chunks	3 to 4	
Spinach, fresh	2 to 3	
Squash, fall, 1-inch chunks	4 to 6	
Squash, summer, sliced	1 to 2	
Sweet potato, 1½-inch chunks	4 to 5	
Turnips, sliced	2 to 3	

Steaming Your Vegetables

Most pressure cookers come with a trivet and steaming basket or rack, all shown in Figure 9-1. These enable you to steam vegetables in a matter of minutes as opposed to boiling them in water the old, conventional way. In fact, with a pressure cooker and steamer basket or rack, you'll never, ever have to cook vegetables by drowning them in boiling water again! To use these nifty accessories, simply pour 2 to 3 cups of water into the pressure cooker pot. Place the trivet in the pot. Position the steaming basket or rack on the trivet and add the vegetables. Most steaming racks simply sit on the bottom of the pressure cooker, lip side down. Add the water and veggies. If your pressure cooker didn't come with a steaming basket or rack, you can purchase an adjustable stainless steel one in the gadget section of most housewares stores and some supermarkets. Start the countdown time for cooking once the pressure cooker reaches and maintains high pressure (see Table 9-1 for cooking times).

When you're done cooking, simply remove the vegetables by removing the steaming basket with a potholder and pulling up on the basket handle. If you're using a steaming rack, remove the vegetables with a slotted spoon.

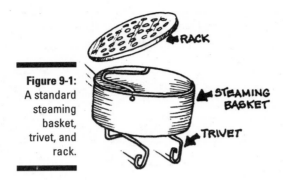

Figure 9-1:
A standard steaming basket, trivet, and rack.

Casseroles

Casseroles are great when made in the pressure cooker. As an example, I include one of my favorite show-off side dishes — Cauliflower and Broccoli Custard — in this chapter. I used to make this casserole dish in the oven, in a hot water bath (see Chapter 10 for a complete description of hot water baths). One day I was really pressed for time. Because I had begun to make cheesecakes in the pressure cooker and the final "baking" steps really weren't all that different, I decided to come up with a pressure cooker method for making custard-based casseroles such as the one in this chapter as well as a custardy corn pudding and others. The results were excellent, and it was great not having to turn the oven on for a single side dish.

Eat Those Veggies!

Vegetables should be a part of every meal. In fact, you should eat at least seven servings of fruits and vegetables every day for a healthy diet. To help you get going, I share with you some of my favorite vegetable recipes for both hot and cold dishes.

☙ Grandma's Mashed Potatoes

Homemade, real mashed potatoes are comfort food with a capital C. Whether you like them creamy or lumpy, mashed potatoes are the perfect accompaniment to any entree, especially when there's lots of savory gravy to spoon on top.

Preparation time: _10 minutes_

Cooking time: _7 minutes under pressure_

Pressure level: _High_

Yield: _4 servings_

3 cups water	_6 tablespoons butter_
4 medium-large russet potatoes, peeled and cut into 1½-inch chunks	_Salt and pepper to taste_
¼ to ½ cup milk	

1 Pour the water into a pressure cooker. Place the potatoes in a steaming basket and place in the pressure cooker.

2 Cover and bring to high pressure over high heat. Lower the heat to stabilize the pressure. Cook for 7 minutes.

3 Remove from the heat. Release the pressure with a quick-release method.

4 Unlock and remove the cover. Taste the potatoes. If they're still hard, return to Step 2 and cook for an additional 1 to 2 minutes.

5 Carefully remove the steaming basket with the potatoes. Discard the cooking liquid.

6 Place the milk and 5 tablespoons of the butter in the pressure cooker. Heat the milk, uncovered, over medium-high heat until the butter melts. Remove from the heat. Add the potatoes and mash, using a hand-held potato masher or electric mixer, until creamy. Season with salt and pepper.

7 Spoon into a large serving bowl. Make an indentation on top of the potatoes with a large spoon. Top with the remaining 1 tablespoon butter. Serve immediately.

Vary It! _To make Garlic Mashed Potatoes, add 5 cloves of peeled, crushed garlic along with the raw potatoes. To make Cheddar Cheese and Chives Mashed Potatoes, add ½ cup of grated extra-sharp cheddar cheese and 3 tablespoons of snipped fresh chives before serving._

Per serving: _Calories 289 (From Fat 161); Fat 18g (Saturated 11g); Cholesterol 49mg; Sodium 161mg; Carbohydrate 30g (Dietary Fiber 3g); Protein 3g._

⏲ Bubble and Squeak

A curious name for a vegetable dish, Bubble and Squeak is a traditional recipe from the British Isles that's a delicious combination of mashed potatoes, braised cabbage, and buttery, sautéed scallions. It derives its name from the noise it makes as it slowly simmers and bubbles during the last few moments of cooking.

Preparation time: _20 minutes_

Cooking time: _11 minutes under pressure_

Pressure level: _High_

Yield: _6 servings_

3 cups water

½ small head green cabbage (about 1 pound), cored and coarsely chopped

2 pounds (about 4 medium) all-purpose potatoes

4 tablespoons butter

8 scallions, white and light green parts, thinly sliced

1 cup milk

Salt and pepper to taste

2 tablespoons minced flat-leaf Italian parsley

1 Pour the water into a pressure cooker. Place the cabbage in a steaming basket and place in the pressure cooker.

2 Cover and bring to high pressure. Lower the heat to stabilize pressure. Cook for 4 minutes.

3 Remove from the heat. Release the pressure with a quick-release method.

4 Unlock and remove the cover. Carefully remove the steaming basket with the cabbage. Place the cabbage in a bowl and set aside.

5 Place the potatoes in the steaming basket and place in the pressure cooker.

6 Cover and bring to high pressure. Lower the heat to stabilize the pressure. Cook for 7 minutes.

7 Remove from the heat. Release the pressure with a quick-release method.

8 Unlock and remove the cover. Taste the potatoes. If they're still hard, return to Step 6 and cook for an additional 1 to 2 minutes.

9 Carefully remove the steaming basket with the potatoes. Discard the cooking liquid. Rinse out the pot and dry. Melt the butter over medium heat. Add the scallions and cook until softened but not browned, about 2 minutes. Reduce the heat to low. Add the cooked potatoes. With a potato masher or fork, mash until smooth. Add the cooked cabbage, and milk, stirring until heated through. Season with salt and black pepper.

10 Spoon into a serving bowl and sprinkle with the parsley.

**Per serving:** Calories 221 (From Fat 85); Fat 9g (Saturated 6g); Cholesterol 26mg; Sodium 420mg; Carbohydrate 31g (Dietary Fiber 4g); Protein 5g.

⏺ Candied Yams

I always thought that I didn't like candied yams, but what I really didn't like was the canned variety. Once I tried homemade candied yams, I was amazed how delicious they really are.

Preparation time: *10 minutes*

Cooking time: *7 minutes under pressure*

Pressure level: *High*

Yield: *8 servings*

2 strips orange peel	*¾ teaspoon ground cinnamon*
3 pounds small yams, peeled and cut into ½-inch thick slices	*Pinch of salt*
	1 cup orange juice
¾ cup packed light brown sugar	*1 tablespoon butter, softened*

1 Place the orange peel in the bottom of a pressure cooker. Add the sweet potato slices in three layers, sprinkling each layer with one-third of the the brown sugar and cinnamon, ending with a final layer of brown sugar and cinnamon. Sprinkle with salt and drizzle with the orange juice. Dot with the butter.

2 Cover and bring to high pressure over high heat. Lower the heat to stabilize the pressure. Cook for 7 minutes.

3 Remove from the heat. Release the pressure with a quick-release method.

4 Unlock and remove the cover. Taste the yams. If they're still hard, return to Step 2 and cook for an additional 1 to 2 minutes.

5 Carefully remove the candied yams with a spatula to a serving bowl. Discard the orange peel. Bring the cooking liquid in the pressure cooker to a boil, and cook until the liquid is reduced by half. Pour the syrup over the yams.

Per serving: Calories 141 (From Fat 14); Fat 2g (Saturated 1g); Cholesterol 4mg; Sodium 30mg; Carbohydrate 32g (Dietary Fiber 1g); Protein 1g.

◎ Mashed Butternut Squash and Parsnips

Butternut squash and parsnips are ideal winter vegetables for steaming and mashing together. The squash gives a beautiful orange color and soft texture to the dish, while the parsnips impart a pleasantly sweet flavor.

Preparation time: *10 minutes*

Cooking time: *5 minutes under pressure*

Pressure level: *High*

Yield: *6 to 8 servings*

3 cups water

1 pound parsnips, peeled and cut into 1-inch chunks

2 pounds butternut squash, seeded, peeled, and cut into 1-inch chunks

½ cup milk

4 tablespoons butter

2 tablespoons light brown sugar

Salt and pepper to taste

1 Pour the water into a pressure cooker. Place the parsnips and squash in the pressure cooker.

2 Cover and bring to high pressure over high heat. Lower the heat to stabilize the pressure. Cook for 5 minutes.

3 Remove from the heat. Release the pressure with a quick-release method.

4 Unlock and remove the cover. Taste the vegetables. If they're still hard, return to Step 2 and cook for an additional 1 to 2 minutes.

5 Carefully remove the steaming basket with the vegetables. Discard the cooking liquid.

6 Place the milk, butter, and brown sugar in the pressure cooker. Heat, uncovered, over medium-high heat until the butter melts. Remove from the heat. Add the vegetables and mash, using a hand-held potato masher or electric mixer, until creamy. Season with salt and pepper. Serve immediately.

Per serving: Calories 149 (From Fat 59); Fat 7g (Saturated 4g); Cholesterol 18mg; Sodium 231mg; Carbohydrate 23g (Dietary Fiber 4g); Protein 2g.

⟡ Coral and Pearls

This dish bears a very poetic name for some very simple vegetables. The elongated pieces of carrots remind me of pieces of orange coral amongst the pearl white onions, and the two vegetables are a nice contrast to each other. I like to serve this dish with grilled or roasted pork, lamb, or poultry.

Preparation time: *15 minutes*

Cooking time: *2 minutes under pressure*

Pressure level: *High*

Yield: *4 servings*

3 cups water

2 pounds of the smallest baby carrots you can find

1 pint white pearl onions, peeled

2 tablespoons butter

2 tablespoons light brown sugar

Salt and pepper to taste

1 tablespoon snipped fresh dill

1 Pour the water into a pressure cooker. Place the carrots and onions in a steaming basket and place in the pressure cooker.

2 Cover and bring to high pressure over high heat. Lower the heat to stabilize the pressure. Cook for 2 minutes.

3 Remove from the heat. Release the pressure with a quick-release method.

4 Unlock and remove the cover.

5 Carefully remove the steaming basket with the vegetables. Discard the cooking liquid. Rinse and wipe the pressure cooker dry.

6 Place the butter and brown sugar in the pressure cooker. Melt the butter over medium heat, stirring until the sugar is melted. Add the carrots and onions. Stir until coated with sugar. Cook until lightly caramelized and soft, about 5 minutes. Season with salt and pepper. Place in a serving bowl and sprinkle with the dill.

Tip: For a quick and easy way to peel small pearl onions, trim the root end and drop the onions in boiling water for 30 to 45 seconds. Immediately rinse under cold water and slip the skins off.

Per serving: Calories 229 (From Fat 64); Fat 7g (Saturated 4g); Cholesterol 16mg; Sodium 247mg; Carbohydrate 40g (Dietary Fiber 5g); Protein 3g.

◔ *Cauliflower and Broccoli Custard*

This vegetable dish is delicious and quite easy to make, so don't be put off by what may appear to be a lengthy list of steps. It's almost puddinglike when it's done cooking. One taste and you'll definitely be coming back for more.

Preparation time: *30 minutes*

Cooking time: *28 minutes under pressure*

Pressure level: *High*

Yield: *8 servings*

6 cups water

1 small head cauliflower, trimmed and broken into florets

1 small bunch broccoli, trimmed and cut into florets

4 tablespoons butter

6 tablespoons flour

1½ cups milk

1 teaspoon salt

⅛ teaspoon pepper

Pinch of nutmeg

6 eggs

⅔ cup grated Parmesan cheese

Salt and pepper to taste

1 Pour 3 cups of the water into a pressure cooker. Place the cauliflower in a steaming basket and place in the pressure cooker.

2 Cover and bring to high pressure over high heat. Lower the heat to stabilize the pressure. Cook for 4 minutes.

3 Remove from the heat. Release the pressure with a quick-release method.

4 Unlock and remove the cover.

5 Carefully remove the cauliflower to a large bowl. Place the broccoli in the steaming basket.

6 Cover and bring to high pressure over high heat. Lower the heat to stabilize the pressure. Cook for 4 minutes.

7 Remove from the heat. Release the pressure with a quick-release method.

8 Unlock and remove the cover.

9 Puree the cauliflower in a food processor and place in a large mixing bowl. Puree the broccoli in a food processor and place in a large mixing bowl. Wash and dry the pressure cooker. Set aside.

10 To prepare a white sauce, melt the butter in a saucepan over medium heat. Stir in the flour and cook for 2 minutes. Whisk in the milk, 1 teaspoon salt, ⅛ teaspoon pepper, and nutmeg. Simmer for 5 minutes.

11 Add half the white sauce to each of the vegetable purees. Add 3 beaten eggs and ⅓ cup Parmesan cheese to each vegetable puree. Season with salt and pepper.

12 Butter a 2-quart soufflé dish that fits in the pressure cooker. Pour the cauliflower mixture into the prepared dish. Spoon the broccoli mixture on top. With a flat knife, swirl the mixture to give it a marbelized affect. Cover the top of the dish with foil.

13 Place a metal trivet or round rack in the bottom of the pressure cooker. Pour in the remaining 3 cups of water. Fold a 24-inch length of foil in half lengthwise (see the related figure in Chapter 10). Center the foil strip on the trivet, molding it on the trivet and up the sides of the pressure cooker. Place the prepared custard in the pressure cooker. Fold the ends of the aluminum foil strip on top of the dish.

14 Cover and bring to high pressure over high heat. Lower the heat to stabilize the pressure. Cook for 20 minutes.

15 Remove from the heat. Release the pressure with a quick-release method.

16 Unlock and remove the cover. Let the custard cool a few minutes. To remove the dish from the pressure cooker, pull up on the ends of the aluminum foil strips.

Per serving: Calories 223 (From Fat 124); Fat 14g (Saturated 7g); Cholesterol 188mg; Sodium 549mg; Carbohydrate 13g (Dietary Fiber 3g); Protein 13g.

◌ *Steamed Lemon Artichokes*

Did you know that artichokes are the flower bud of the artichoke plant? A favorite ingredient in most Mediterranean cuisines, depending on their size, artichokes can be prepared by braising, stuffing, frying, roasting, or steaming, which is what you do in this recipe. Serve with a lemon dipping sauce.

Preparation time: *15 minutes*

Cooking time: *7 minutes under pressure*

Pressure level: *High*

Yield: *4 servings*

1 cup water

Juice of 2 lemons, rinds reserved

1 teaspoon salt

1 bay leaf

4 large artichokes

1 cup mayonnaise

1 clove garlic, peeled and minced

2 tablespoons minced flat-leaf Italian parsley, or snipped dill

1 Pour the water into a pressure cooker. Add all but 3 tablespoons of the lemon juice, the salt, and bay leaf. Stir until the salt disolves. Place the reserved lemon rinds in the water.

2 Cut off the stems from the artichokes. (See Figure 9-2.) Tear off and discard the top two or three layers of tough outer leaves. Cut off 1 to 1½ inches from the tops of the artichokes. Carefully open and expose the inner leaves and choke. Pull out and remove any thorny leaves. With a teaspoon, scoop out and discard any fuzzy matter from the center choke. Wet artichokes in the lemon water in the pressure cooker to slow down discoloring. Place upside down in a steaming basket in the pressure cooker.

3 Cover and bring to high pressure over high heat. Lower the heat to stabilize the pressure. Cook for 7 minutes.

4 Remove from the heat. Release the pressure with a quick-release method.

5 Unlock and remove the cover. Carefully remove the artichokes from the pressure cooker with a slotted spoon and cool to room temperature.

6 In a small mixing bowl, whisk together the mayonnaise, the remaining 3 tablespoons of lemon juice, and the garlic.

7 Carefully open the center of each artichoke and fill with one-fourth of the lemon mayonnaise. Sprinke the tops with the parsley or dill.

8 Pluck artichoke leaves from whole artichoke. Dip them into the lemon mayonnaise. Eat by scraping the underside of the leaves along your upper teeth to remove the soft flesh; discard the leaf. The center leaves are usually tender enough to be eaten whole.

Per serving: *Calories 457 (From Fat 396); Fat 44g (Saturated 7g); Cholesterol 33mg; Sodium 712mg; Carbohydrate 15g (Dietary Fiber 7g); Protein 5g.*

PREPARING AN ARTICHOKE

1. CUT OFF STEMS FROM THE ARTICHOKES. TEAR OFF AND DISCARD THE TOP TWO OR THREE LAYERS OF TOUGH, OUTER LEAVES.

2. CAREFULLY, OPEN AND EXPOSE INNER LEAVES AND 'CHOKE.' PULL OUT AND REMOVE ANY THORNY LEAVES.

3. WITH A TEASPOON, SCOOP OUT AND DISCARD ANY FUZZY MATTER FROM THE CENTER CHOKE.

4. WET ARTICHOKES IN THE LEMON WATER IN THE PRESSURE COOKER TO SLOW DOWN ANY DISCOLORING.

5. PLACE UPSIDE DOWN IN THE STEAMING BASKET IN THE PRESSURE COOKER.

Figure 9-2: Preparing artichokes for cooking.

Greens in Pot Likker

Greens is the name that some folks give to kale, mustard, collard, and turnip or beet tops. While humble in nature and appearance, these leafy green vegetables are full of flavor and high in minerals and vitamins. Although you can make them with a tablespoon or two of olive oil, I've opted for the traditional version made with a small piece of salt pork for flavor. Serve with some of the cooking liquid, or pot likker, as it's commonly called.

Preparation time: *10 minutes*

Cooking time: *5 minutes under pressure*

Pressure level: *High*

Yield: *6 to 8 servings*

4-ounce piece of salt pork

1 bunch (about 1 pound) of greens, such as kale, mustard, collard, turnip, or beet, rinsed very well, stems removed, coarsely chopped

2 cups water

1 teaspoon sugar

2 pinches of crushed, hot red pepper

Salt and black pepper to taste

1 Brown the salt pork in a pressure cooker over medium heat until golden. Add the greens, water, sugar, and hot pepper.

2 Cover and bring to high pressure over high heat. Lower the heat to stabilize the pressure. Cook for 5 minutes.

3 Remove from the heat. Release the pressure with a quick-release method.

4 Unlock and remove the cover.

5 Season with salt and pepper. Serve the greens in a bowl with some of the pot likker.

Per serving: *Calories 95 (From Fat 75); Fat 8g (Saturated 3g); Cholesterol 9mg; Sodium 222mg; Carbohydrate 4g (Dietary Fiber 1g); Protein 2g.*

Sweet-and-Sour Red Cabbage

This dish is the perfect accompaniment to many German and Northern European dishes. Have a batch on hand to serve with Sauerbraten (Chapter 4) and Caraway Pork Roast (Chapter 7).

Preparation time: *15 minutes*

Cooking time: *6 minutes under pressure*

Pressure level: *High*

Yield: *6 to 8 servings*

2 tablespoons vegetable oil

1 large red onion, chopped

½ cup apple cider vinegar

1 cup chicken stock or broth

½ cup packed dark brown sugar

¼ teaspoon ground cloves

2-pound head red cabbage, tough outer leaves discarded, shredded

2 Granny Smith apples, peeled, cored, and cut into ½-inch chunks

1 bay leaf

Salt and pepper to taste

1 Heat the vegetable oil in a pressure cooker over medium-high heat. Add the onion and cook until soft. Add the vinegar, chicken stock, brown sugar, and cloves. Stir well until the sugar disolves. Add the cabbage, apple chunks, and bay leaf.

2 Cover and bring to high pressure over high heat. Lower the heat to stabilize the pressure. Cook for 6 minutes.

3 Remove from the heat. Release the pressure with a quick-release method.

4 Unlock and remove the cover. Taste the cabbage. If it's not tender, return to Step 2 and cook for an additional 1 to 2 minutes. Remove and discard the bay leaf. Season to taste.

Per serving: Calories 138 (From Fat 38); Fat 4g (Saturated 0g); Cholesterol 1mg; Sodium 213mg; Carbohydrate 26g (Dietary Fiber 3g); Protein 2g.

ᗱ Pickled Beets

Every recipe I have ever read for pickled beets cooks the beets first and then pickles them for up to 24 hours before eating. Because the pressure cooker infuses the food with whatever cooking liquid is being used, I decided to experiment and see whether I could cook and pickle the beets in one easy step. The results are delicious!

Preparation time: *20 minutes*

Cooking time: *3 minutes under pressure*

Pressure level: *High*

Yield: *4 to 6 servings*

1 cup water

½ cup apple cider vinegar

⅓ cup packed dark brown sugar

1 tablespoon pickling spices

1 teaspoon salt

2 pounds beets (about 4 large), peeled and thinly sliced

1 medium red onion, sliced into rings

1 clove garlic, peeled and sliced

1 bay leaf

1 Combine the water, vinegar, brown sugar, pickling spices, and salt in the pressure cooker. Stir until the sugar disolves. Add the beets, onions, garlic, and bay leaf.

2 Cover and bring to high pressure. Lower the heat to stabilize the pressure. Cook for 3 minutes.

3 Remove from the heat. Release the pressure with a quick-release method.

4 Unlock and remove the cover. Taste the beets. They should be crisp-tender. If they're too hard, return to Step 2 and cook for 1 additional minute.

5 Carefully remove the beets and onions with a slotted spoon to a bowl. Bring the cooking liquid to a boil and reduce by half. Pour through a strainer over the beets. Cool to room temperature before serving.

Per serving: Calories 114 (From Fat 2); Fat 0g (Saturated 0g); Cholesterol 0mg; Sodium 500mg; Carbohydrate 28g (Dietary Fiber 3g); Protein 2g.

Salade Niçoise

This dish, which originated in Nice, France, is one of my favorite salad entrees to make and eat on those hot, dog days of summer. Because each vegetable is displayed separately on a bed of lettuce, you need and want the best-quality ingredients possible.

Preparation time: *20 minutes*

Cooking time: *7 minutes under pressure*

Pressure level: *High*

Yield: *4 to 6 servings*

3 cups water

1 pound green beans, trimmed and cut into 1½-inch pieces

1 pound small red or new potatoes, scrubbed well and pricked twice with a fork

4 eggs

1 large head Boston or green leaf lettuce, washed and dried

2 cans (7 ounces each) oil-packed tuna

1 pint cherry tomatoes

1 cucumber, peeled and cut into ¼-inch slices

½ cup brine-cured black olives

1 small red onion, sliced into thin rings

4 tablespoons extra-virgin olive oil

4 tablespoons red wine vinegar

1 tablespoon Dijon mustard

¼ teaspoon dried thyme

Salt and pepper to taste

1 Pour the water into a pressure cooker. Place the green beans, potatoes, and eggs in a steaming basket and place in the pressure cooker.

2 Cover and bring to high pressure over high heat. Lower the heat to stabilize the pressure. Cook for 7 minutes.

3 Remove from the heat. Release the pressure with a quick-release method.

4 Unlock and remove the cover. Taste the potatoes. If they're still hard, return to Step 2 and cook for an additional 1 to 2 minutes.

5 Carefully remove the steaming basket with the vegetables and eggs. Remove the eggs and potatoes; peel and quarter.

6 Line a serving platter with the lettuce. Mound the green beans on one half of the platter and the potatoes on the other. Mound the tuna in the center. Place the eggs, tomatoes, cucumbers, and black olives around the beans and potatoes. Place the onion slices on top of the salad.

7 Whisk together the olive oil, vinegar, mustard, and thyme. Season with the salt and pepper. Drizzle on top of the salad and serve immediately.

Per serving: *Calories 357 (From Fat 178); Fat 20g (Saturated 3g); Cholesterol 152mg; Sodium 537mg; Carbohydrate 21g (Dietary Fiber 5g); Protein 25g.*

❦ Warm French-Style Potato Salad

This simple-to-make potato salad from France is a delicious departure from the all too familiar mayonnaise variety.

Preparation time: *15 minutes*

Cooking time: *7 minutes under pressure*

Pressure level: *High*

Yield: *4 servings*

1½ cups dry white wine

¼ cup white wine vinegar

1 teaspoon salt

2 pounds small red or new potatoes, scrubbed well and pricked twice with a fork

4 tablespoons extra-virgin olive oil

2 tablespoons chopped flat-leaf Italian parsley

Salt and pepper to taste

4 scallions, white and green parts, thinly sliced

1 Combine the white wine, vinegar, and 1 teaspoon salt in the pressure cooker. Add the potatoes.

2 Cover and bring to high pressure. Lower the heat to stabilize the pressure. Cook for 7 minutes.

3 Remove from the heat. Release the pressure with a quick-release method.

4 Unlock and remove the cover. Taste the potatoes. If they're still hard, return to Step 2 and cook for an additional 1 to 2 minutes.

5 Carefully remove the potatoes with a slotted spoon to a colander. Quarter the potatoes and place in a large bowl.

6 Bring the cooking liquid to a boil and reduce by half. Pour into a small mixing bowl. Add the olive oil and parsley. Whisk together. Season with salt and pepper. Pour over the potatoes. Add the scallions and toss gently.

Per serving: Calories 281 (From Fat 124); Fat 14g (Saturated 2g); Cholesterol 0mg; Sodium 738mg; Carbohydrate 32g (Dietary Fiber 5g); Protein 6g.

☉ *Ratatouille*

Ratatouille is a hearty vegetable stew from the Provence region of France. It is made with the brightly colored and flavorful vegetables the area is known for. This dish is hearty enough to be served as a main course with salad, cheese, and crusty bread, but you can also serve it as a side dish with grilled meats or fish.

Preparation time: *20 minutes*

Cooking time: *4 minutes under pressure*

Pressure level: *High*

Yield: *4 to 6 servings*

3 tablespoons olive oil	*½ teaspoon dried thyme*
1 medium onion, chopped	*1½ teaspoons salt*
2 cloves garlic, peeled and thinly sliced	*¼ teaspoon black pepper*
1 green bell pepper, cored, seeded, and diced	*1 large eggplant, peeled and cut into ½-inch cubes (see Figure 9-3)*
1 red bell pepper, cored, seeded, and diced	*2 tablespoons shredded basil*
1 small zucchini, trimmed, quartered lengthwise, and diced	*2 tablespoons minced flat-leaf Italian parsley*
1 can (14½ ounces) diced tomatoes	*Salt and pepper to taste*
¼ cup water	*2 tablespoons red wine vinegar*

1 Heat the olive oil in a pressure cooker over medium-high heat. Add the onion, garlic, and the green and red bell peppers. Cook until the onion is soft.

2 Add the zucchini, tomatoes, water, thyme, 1½ teaspoons salt, and ¼ teaspoon black pepper. Cook for 2 minutes. Add the eggplant.

3 Cover and bring to high pressure over high heat. Lower the heat to stabilize the pressure. Cook for 4 minutes.

4 Remove from the heat. Release the pressure with a quick-release method.

5 Unlock and remove the cover. Add the basil and parsley. Season with salt and black pepper. Stir in the vinegar. Serve hot or at room temperature.

Per serving: *Calories 121 (From Fat 64); Fat 7g (Saturated 1g); Cholesterol 0mg; Sodium 771mg; Carbohydrate 15g (Dietary Fiber 5g); Protein 2g.*

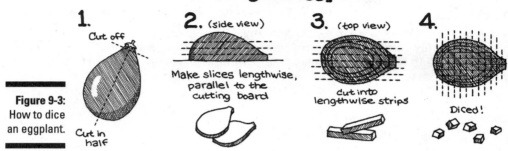

Figure 9-3:
How to dice
an eggplant.

Chapter 10

Desserts, Jams, and Chutneys

● ●

In This Chapter

▶ Giving your desserts a hot water bath

▶ Making luscious jams and fruit dishes

● ●

Some people shy away from making desserts because they think it takes too long. Nothing could be further from the truth when it comes to the pressure cooker. Creamy cheesecakes, like the ones most people only dream about, are ready from start to finish in 35 minutes. Smooth egg custard and homey apple crisp are ready in even less time. Get the picture? Now get going and start turning out your own post-dinner extravaganzas!

The Pressure Cooker as a Hot Water Bath

I'm sure that you've made a recipe or two in your lifetime that called for a *bain-marie,* which is French for "hot water bath." Certain desserts, such as cheesecake and baked custard, for example, should not brown as they cook. To prevent browning, they are baked at a moderately high temperature with the cake or baking pan sitting in a larger pan of simmering water.

Well, imagine your pressure cooker as an enclosed *bain-marie* that cooks up 70 percent faster than your oven. By placing a cheesecake or pudding, for example, on a trivet sitting over simmer water in a steam bath environment in the pressure cooker, you can make some great desserts.

You should know a couple things about this technique before trying your hand at it. Some pressure cookers come with a steamer basket and trivet set or a steamer plate. The trivet or steamer plate is essential when "baking" in your pressure cooker. If you don't have one, purchase a 6- to 7-inch round, wire, metal cooling rack with legs at your favorite housewares store. The best type of pan to use when making a cheesecake in your pressure cooker is a 7-inch springform pan with removable sides. So that you don't run the risk of water leaking into the pan, cover the bottom and sides with one sheet of aluminum foil.

Most of you probably have different-sized casserole and baking dishes in your kitchen. Small, deep, round ones work the best when making dishes such as bread pudding and crisps.

Always make sure that the baking dish or pan you use is heatproof and small enough to fit in your pressure cooker. To make it easier to position and later remove the dish or pan, make an aluminum foil sling to assist you, as shown in Figure 10-1.

The sling is simply made from a 24-inch long sheet of aluminum foil, folded in half lengthwise. Once the foil is folded, you center the prepared, covered pan of food on the sling. Holding the ends of the sling, carefully lower the pan into the pressure cooker onto the trivet (the one that came with the steaming basket) or onto a small, round metal wire cooling rack (7 inches in diameter or smaller to fit into the pressure cooker). The ends of the sling are folded down on top of the pan of food. To remove the cooked pan of food, carefully pull up on the ends of the sling.

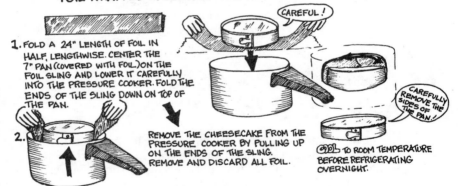

FOIL-WRAPPED CAKE PAN WITH FOIL SLING AND TRIVET

1. FOLD A 24" LENGTH OF FOIL IN HALF, LENGTHWISE. CENTER THE 7" PAN (COVERED WITH FOIL) ON THE FOIL SLING AND LOWER IT CAREFULLY INTO THE PRESSURE COOKER. FOLD THE ENDS OF THE SLING DOWN ON TOP OF THE PAN.

CAREFUL!

2. REMOVE THE CHEESECAKE FROM THE PRESSURE COOKER BY PULLING UP ON THE ENDS OF THE SLING. REMOVE AND DISCARD ALL FOIL.

CAREFULLY REMOVE THE SIDES OF THE PAN!

COOL TO ROOM TEMPERATURE BEFORE REFRIGERATING OVERNIGHT.

Figure 10-1:
Making and using an aluminum foil sling.

To prevent wet tops on baked goods, securely cover the pan or baking dish with a sheet of aluminum foil before placing it in the pressure cooker.

Cheesecakes and Other Tasty Desserts

Cheesecakes, custards, and puddings were made for the pressure cooker. Although these desserts are usually baked in the oven in a hot water bath, they bake wonderfully in the hot water bath atmosphere that the pressure cooker creates. The addition of hot, intense steam adds greater benefit because everything winds up cooking at least 50 percent faster, too.

Chocolate Sandwich Cookie Cheesecake

The following recipe combines America's favorite cookie with one of its favorite desserts: cheesecake.

Preparation time: *15 minutes*

Cooking time: *20 minutes under pressure*

Pressure setting: *High*

Yield: *6 servings*

¾ cup crushed chocolate sandwich cookies

2 tablespoons butter, melted

2 packages (8 ounces each) cream cheese, softened

½ cup sugar

½ teaspoon vanilla

2 eggs

10 chocolate sandwich cookies, quartered

2½ cups water

1 Lightly butter a 7-inch springform pan. Cover the outside bottom and sides of the pan with a single sheet of aluminum foil.

2 Combine the cookie crumbs and melted butter and press into the bottom and 1 inch up the sides of the pan.

3 In a large mixing bowl, mix the cream cheese, sugar, and vanilla with an electric mixer on medium speed until fluffy. Add the eggs, one at a time, mixing on low speed just until well blended. Gently stir in the quartered cookies. Pour over the crust. Cover tightly with aluminum foil.

4 Place a metal trivet or rack in the pressure cooker pot. Pour in the water.

5 Fold a 24-inch length of foil in half lengthwise. Center the pan on the foil sling and carefully lower it into the pressure cooker. Fold the ends of the sling down on top of the pan.

6 Cover and bring to high pressure over high heat. Lower the heat to stabilize the pressure. Cook for 20 minutes.

7 Remove from the heat. Let sit undisturbed for 10 minutes. Release any remaining pressure with a quick-release method.

8 Unlock and remove the cover. Remove the cheesecake from the pressure cooker by pulling up on the ends of the aluminum foil sling. Remove and discard all foil. Cool to room temperature before refrigerating overnight. Before serving, carefully remove the sides of the springform pan.

Per serving: Calories 547 (From Fat 344); Fat 38g (Saturated 21g); Cholesterol 164mg; Sodium 497mg; Carbohydrate 43g (Dietary Fiber 1g); Protein 10g.

Key Lime Cheesecake

Key limes are native to the Florida Keys. Yellow in color, they're much smaller than the more common green Persian lime. If you spot Key limes at a specialty grocer, by all means snap them up for this recipe (shown on the front cover). If not, regular green limes will do, with equally delicious results!

Preparation time: *15 minutes*

Cooking time: *20 minutes under pressure*

Pressure setting: *High*

Yield: *6 servings*

¾ cup graham cracker crumbs

½ cup plus 2 tablespoons sugar

2 tablespoons butter, melted

2 packages (8 ounces each) cream cheese, softened

2 eggs

3 tablespoons freshly squeezed Key or Persian lime juice

2 teaspoons grated lime zest

2½ cups water

1 Lightly butter a 7-inch springform pan. Cover the outside bottom and sides with a single sheet of aluminum foil.

2 Combine the graham cracker crumbs, the 2 tablespoons sugar, and melted butter and press into the bottom and 1 inch up the sides of the pan.

3 In a large mixing bowl, mix the cream cheese and the ½ cup sugar with an electric mixer on medium speed until fluffy. Add the eggs, one at a time, mixing on low speed. Add the lime juice and lime zest and mix until well blended. Pour over the crust. Cover tightly with aluminum foil.

4 Place a metal trivet or rack in the pressure cooker. Pour in the water.

5 Fold a 24-inch length of foil in half lengthwise. Center the pan on the foil sling and carefully lower it into the pressure cooker. Fold the ends of the sling down on top of the pan.

6 Cover and bring to high pressure over high heat. Lower the heat to stabilize the pressure. Cook for 20 minutes.

7 Remove from the heat. Let sit undisturbed 10 minutes. Release any remaining pressure with a quick-release method.

8 Unlock and remove the cover. Remove the cheesecake from the pressure cooker by pulling up on the ends of the aluminum foil sling. Remove and discard all foil. Cool to room temperature before refrigerating overnight. Before serving, carefully remove the sides of the springform pan.

Per serving: Calories 469 (From Fat 301); Fat 33g (Saturated 20g); Cholesterol 164mg; Sodium 336mg; Carbohydrate 35g (Dietary Fiber 1g); Protein 9g.

Double Chocolate Cheesecake

I like anything made from with chocolate, especially this creamy chocolate cheesecake. With a chocolate cookie crust and smooth chocolate filling, this dessert is sure to satisfy the most powerful of chocolate cravings.

Preparation time: *15 minutes*

Cooking time: *20 minutes under pressure*

Pressure setting: *High*

Yield: *6 servings*

¾ cup chocolate wafer cookie crumbs	3 eggs
2 tablespoons butter, melted	1½ cups semisweet chocolate chips, melted in the microwave
2 packages (8 ounces each) cream cheese, softened	1 teaspoon vanilla
½ cup sweetened condensed milk	2½ cups water

1 Lightly butter a 7-inch springform pan. Cover the outside bottom and sides with a single sheet of aluminum foil.

2 Combine the cookie crumbs and melted butter and press into the bottom and 1 inch up the sides of the pan.

3 In a large mixing bowl, mix the cream cheese and condensed milk with an electric mixer on medium speed until fluffy. Add the eggs, one at a time, mixing on low speed. Add the melted chocolate and vanilla and mix until well bleneded. Pour over the crust. Cover tightly with aluminum foil.

4 Place a metal trivet or rack in the pressure cooker. Pour in the water.

5 Fold a 24-inch length of foil in half lengthwise. Center the pan on the foil sling and carefully lower it into the pressure cooker. Fold the ends of the sling down on top of the pan.

6 Cover and bring to high pressure over high heat. Lower the heat to stabilize the pressure. Cook for 20 minutes.

7 Remove from the heat. Let sit undisturbed for 10 minutes. Release any remaining pressure with a quick-release method.

8 Unlock and remove the cover. Remove the cheesecake from the pressure cooker by pulling up on the ends of the aluminum foil sling. Remove and discard all foil. Cool to room temperature before refrigerating overnight. Before serving,carefully remove the sides of the springform pan.

Per serving: Calories 698 (From Fat 446); Fat 50g (Saturated 28g); Cholesterol 208mg; Sodium 375mg; Carbohydrate 55g (Dietary Fiber 1g); Protein 12g.

Italian Ricotta Cheesecake

This cheesecake is different from the others in that it is made with ricotta rather than cream cheese. Traditionally flavored with orange, this cheesecake is the perfect ending to an Italian meal, especially when served with espresso and sambuca, a licorice-flavored liqueur.

Preparation time: *15 minutes*

Cooking time: *20 minutes under pressure*

Pressure setting: *High*

Yield: *6 servings*

¾ cup graham cracker crumbs

⅔ cup plus 2 tablespoons sugar

2 tablespoons butter, melted

1 container (15 ounces) whole-milk ricotta cheese

1 tablespoon grated orange zest

1 teaspoon vanilla

2 tablespoons all-purpose flour

Pinch of salt

3 eggs

¼ cup diced candied orange peel

2½ cups water

Confectioners' sugar

1 Lightly butter a 7-inch springform pan. Cover the outside bottom and sides with a single sheet of aluminum foil.

2 Combine the graham cracker crumbs, the 2 tablespoons sugar, and melted butter and press into the bottom of the pan.

3 In a large mixing bowl, mix the ricotta cheese, orange zest, vanilla, flour, the ⅔ cup sugar, and salt with an electric mixer on medium speed until creamy. Add the eggs, one at a time, mixing on low speed until well blended. Stir in the candied orange peel. Pour over the crust. Cover tightly with aluminum foil.

4 Place a metal trivet or rack in the pressure cooker. Pour in the water.

5 Fold a 24-inch length of foil in half lengthwise. Center the pan on the foil sling and carefully lower it into the pressure cooker. Fold the ends of the sling down on top of the pan.

6 Cover and bring to high pressure over high heat. Lower the heat to stabilize the pressure. Cook for 20 minutes.

7 Remove from the heat. Let sit undisturbed for 10 minutes. Release any remaining pressure with a quick-release method.

8 Unlock and remove the cover. Remove the cheesecake from the pressure cooker by pulling up on the ends of the aluminum foil sling. Remove and discard all foil. Cool to room temperature before refrigerating overnight. Before serving, carefully remove the sides of the springform pan. Sprinkle liberally with confectioners' sugar.

Per serving: Calories 398 (From Fat 154); Fat 17g (Saturated 9g); Cholesterol 152mg; Sodium 206mg; Carbohydrate 49g (Dietary Fiber 1g); Protein 12g

Flan

If Spain had a national dessert, it would undoubtedly be flan, a smooth yet dense egg custard. What makes flan unique is that it cooks in a baking dish on a coating of hardened burnt sugar, which melts into a delicious, caramel-flavored liquid that coats the flan when it is inverted onto a serving plate.

Preparation time: *10 minutes*

Cooking time: *10 minutes under pressure*

Pressure setting: *High*

Yield: *6 servings*

½ cup sugar	⅛ teaspoon salt
1 cup milk	4 eggs, lightly beaten
1 can (14 ounces) sweetened condensed milk	2½ cups water
1 teaspoon vanilla	

1 Heat the sugar in a small skillet over medium heat until it melts and becomes a golden brown syrup. Immediately pour into a 5-cup baking dish that will fit in the pressure cooker, tilting the dish so that the sugar coats the entire bottom. Work quickly because the syrup will harden.

2 Combine the milk, condensed milk, vanilla, and salt in a bowl. Add the eggs and whisk until smooth. Pour into the prepared dish. Cover tightly with aluminum foil.

3 Place a metal trivet or rack in the pressure cooker pot. Pour in the water. Fold a 24-inch length of foil in half lengthwise. Center the baking dish on the foil sling and carefully lower it into the pressure cooker. Fold the ends of the sling down on top of the dish.

4 Cover and bring to high pressure over high heat. Lower the heat to stabilize the pressure. Cook for 10 minutes.

5 Remove from the heat. Release the pressure using the natural release method, about 15 to 20 minutes.

6 Unlock and remove the cover. Remove the flan from the pressure cooker by pulling up on the ends of the aluminum foil sling. Remove and discard all foil. Cool to room temperature before refrigerating overnight.

7 To serve, cut around the edge of the dish with a sharp knife. Place a shallow bowl on top of the dish and turn over. Cut into wedges.

Per serving: *Calories 353 (From Fat 94); Fat 10g (Saturated 6g); Cholesterol 170mg; Sodium 195mg; Carbohydrate 55g (Dietary Fiber 0g); Protein 11g.*

Apple Crisp

Whenever I make this dessert, I always put aside some to eat at breakfast the next day because it reminds me of baked granola with fruit. For a bit of variety, you can easily substitute about 1½ pounds ripe peaches or pears for the apples, with equally delicious results.

Preparation time: *10 minutes*

Cooking time: *20 minutes under pressure*

Pressure setting: *High*

Yield: *6 servings*

4 Granny Smith apples, peeled and thinly sliced (see Figure 10-2)

1 tablespoon lemon juice

1 cup old-fashioned oats

¼ cup flour

½ cup packed light brown sugar

1 teaspoon ground cinnamon

½ teaspoon salt

4 tablespoons melted butter

2½ cups water

1 Sprinkle the apples with the lemon juice.

2 Combine the oats, flour, brown sugar, cinnamon, salt, and butter.

3 Layer the apples and the oat mixture, beginning with and ending with the apples, in a 7-inch springform pan or a 2-quart souffle dish that fits in the pressure cooker. Cover the dish tightly with aluminum foil.

4 Place a metal trivet or rack in the pressure cooker. Pour in the water. Fold a 24-inch length of foil in half lenghtwise. Center the baking dish on the foil sling and carefully lower it into the pressure cooker. Fold the ends of the sling down on top of the dish.

5 Cover and bring to high pressure over high heat. Lower the heat to stabilize the pressure. Cook for 20 minutes.

6 Remove from the heat. Release the pressure using a quick-release method.

7 Unlock and remove the cover. Remove the apple crisp from the pressure cooker by pulling up on the ends of the aluminum foil sling. Remove and discard all foil. Serve warm.

Per serving: Calories 283 (From Fat 103); Fat 11g (Saturated 6g); Cholesterol 27mg; Sodium 308mg; Carbohydrate 45g (Dietary Fiber 3g); Protein 3g.

Peeling and Coring an Apple

Figure 10-2: Peel and core your apples to use in apple crisp.

1. Quarter apples

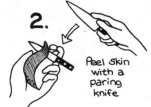

2. Peel skin with a paring knife

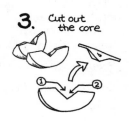

3. Cut out the core

Creamy Rice Pudding

Rice pudding is the queen of comfort desserts. Enjoyed around the world in infinite versions, it is always creamy and soothing and has just enough chew.

Preparation time: *10 minutes*

Cooking time: *10 minutes under pressure*

Pressure setting: *High*

Yield: *6 servings*

2 tablespoons butter	⅓ cup sugar
3 cups milk	1 teaspoon vanilla
1 cup long-grain rice	Ground cinnamon

1 Melt the butter in a pressure cooker over medium-high heat. Add the milk and bring to a boil. Stir in the rice.

2 Cover and bring to high pressure over high heat. Lower the heat to stabilize the pressure. Cook for 10 minutes.

3 Remove from the heat. Release the pressure using the natural release method, about 15 to 25 minutes minutes.

4 Unlock and remove the cover. Stir in the sugar and vanilla. Serve warm or at room temperature, sprinkled with cinnamon.

Per serving: Calories 302 (From Fat 86); Fat 10g (Saturated 6g); Cholesterol 32mg; Sodium 81mg; Carbohydrate 46g (Dietary Fiber 0g); Protein 8g. (using 1 cup rice)

Cinnamon Raisin Bread Pudding

Originally a frugal cook's solution for using up stale bread, bread puddings are a popular, easy-to-prepare dessert. For best results, let the bread absorb as much of the liquid custard as possible before cooking. If you wish, you can substitute the cinnamon raisin bread with any other sweet bread made with dried fruits, spices, and nuts.

Preparation time: 10 minutes

Cooking time: 15 minutes under pressure

Pressure setting: High

Yield: 6 servings

4 slices cinnamon raisin bread, torn into small pieces

2 eggs

1 cans (12 ounces) evaporated milk

½ teaspoon vanilla

¼ teaspoon salt

¼ cup sugar

1 teaspoon butter

Ground cinnamon

2 cups water

1 Butter a 5-cup baking dish that fits in your pressure cooker. Place the bread pieces in the baking dish.

2 Whisk the eggs, milk, vanilla, salt, and sugar together to make a custard. Pour over the bread and let set until the custard is absorbed.

3 Dot the top with the butter. Sprinkle with cinnamon. Cover tightly with aluminum foil.

4 Place a metal trivet or rack in the pressure cooker. Pour in the water. Fold a 24-inch length of foil in half lengthwise. Center the baking dish on the foil sling and carefully lower it into the pressure cooker. Fold the ends of the sling down on top of the dish.

5 Cover and bring to high pressure over high heat. Lower the heat to stabilize the pressure. Cook for 15 minutes.

6 Remove from the heat. Release the pressure using a quick-release method.

7 Unlock and remove the cover. Remove the pudding from the pressure cooker by pulling up on the ends of the aluminum strips. Remove and discard all foil. Serve warm, or cool to room temperature.

Per serving: Calories 333 (From Fat 108); Fat 12g (Saturated 6g); Cholesterol 144mg; Sodium 451mg; Carbohydrate 42g (Dietary Fiber 1g); Protein 13g.

Sparkling Jars of Fruit

Years ago, people would "put up" jars of fruit purees and preserves to take advantage of an abundant harvest and to prepare for the long winter months ahead when fresh fruit wouldn't be available. Even though you now can enjoy fresh fruits year-round, a pint of homemade jam is still always a welcome gift.

Although canning may be a dying art, making quick and easy preserves in your pressure cooker needn't be. Although most fresh fruit preserves require slow simmering, those made with flavor-concentrated dried fruits do exceptionally well in the pressure cooker, as with the fruits I paired up in my jam recipes.

Your 4-, 6-, or 8- quart pressure cooker was designed and manufactured for cooking food and not canning. Much larger than pressure cookers (10 quarts and up), pressure canners are wider in diameter, come with wire baskets for holding canning jars so that they don't rattle and bang into each other, and usually have a dial pressure regulator gauge on the cover that gives you the exact psi as you pressure can food. If pressure canning is what you want to do, I strongly recommend that you obtain or purchase a pressure canner and not use your regular pressure cooker.

Apples are usually very abundant by October. If you haven't had homemade applesauce in a while, reacquaint yourself next autumn and make a batch of my easy-to-make pink applesauce. In fact, don't let yourself be limited by apples and dried fruits. Use the recommended cooking times in Table 10-1 and experiment with whatever ripe fruits, including those shown in Figure 10-3, that catch your eye at your local farm stand or greengrocer.

All cooking times are at best approximations and should be used as general guidelines. Not all types of apples cook for the same amount of time, for example. You may also find that your particular brand or model of pressure cooker cooks faster or even a bit slower. Therefore, feel free to note any cooking time differences in the right-hand column of the table. The cooking times in Table 10-1 begin when the pressure cooker reaches high pressure. Always start with the shortest cooking time; you can always continue cooking under pressure for an additional couple minutes until the desired texture is reached.

Figure 10-3:
Fruit
products
are fabulous
when made
in the
pressure
cooker.

Table 10-1	Recommended Pressure Cooker Cooking Times for Fruits	
Food	*Cooking Time (in Minutes)*	*Your Notes*
Apples, chunks or eighths	4 to 5	
Apples, slices, dried	2 to 3	
Apricots, whole or halved	2 to 3	
Apricots, dried	3 to 4	
Peaches, halved	3 to 4	
Peaches, dried	4 to 5	
Pears, halved	3 to 4	
Pears, dried	4 to 5	
Plums, whole or halved	2 to 3	
Prunes	2 to 3	
Raisins	2 to 3	

Autumn Harvest Applesauce

With a bright pink blush from tart cranberries, this applesauce surely outshines anything from a jar. It's sweetened with fresh apple cider and real maple syrup. Use the crispest of apples for the best flavor and texture.

Preparation time: *10 minutes*

Cooking time: *5 minutes under pressure*

Pressure setting: *High*

Yield: *8 servings*

3 pounds apples, such as Jonathan, Golden Delicious, or Jonagold, peeled, cored, and quartered

1½ cups fresh or frozen cranberries

1 cinnamon stick

1 cup apple cider or apple juice

½ cup real maple syrup

Pinch of salt

1 Place the apples, cranberries, cinnamon stick, cider, maple syrup, and salt in a pressure cooker. Stir well.

2 Cover and bring to high pressure. Lower the heat to stabilize the pressure and cook for 5 minutes.

3 Remove from the heat. Release the pressure using a quick-release method.

4 Unlock and remove the cover. The apples should be very soft. Remove and discard the cinnamon stick.

5 Puree the apples with a handheld potato masher or process with a hand blender in the pressure cooker pot. Taste and add additional maple syrup or sugar, if desired. Refrigerate when cool.

Tip: *Fresh cranberries are available from September through early winter. Because they freeze well for up to a year, buy a few extra bags and store them in your freezer to have a ready supply year-round.*

Per serving: *Calories 159 (From Fat 5); Fat 1g (Saturated 0g); Cholesterol 0mg; Sodium 23mg; Carbohydrate 41g (Dietary Fiber 3g); Protein 0g.*

Apricot-Pineapple Jam

Like a rising sun in the morning, this jam is a beautiful combination of bright orange and golden yellow. It's also an outstanding blend of apricot and pineapple flavors. I especially like to serve this jam with homemade bran and corn muffins for Sunday morning breakfast.

Preparation time: *10 minutes*

Cooking time: *5 minutes under pressure*

Pressure setting: *High*

Yield: *Approximately 4 cups*

1½ cups water

2 tablespoons lemon juice

1 cup sugar

1 pound dried apricots

1 can (20 ounces) crushed pineapple, with juice

1 Bring the water and lemon juice to a boil in a pressure cooker. Add the sugar and stir until dissolved. Add the apricots and pineapple.

2 Cover and bring to high pressure over high heat. Lower the heat to stabilize the pressure. Cook for 5 minutes.

3 Remove from the heat. Release the pressure using a quick-release method.

4 Unlock and remove the cover. Spoon the fruit mixture in a food processor bowl. Process until it's the consistency, from chunky to smooth, that you want. Refrigerate when cool.

Per serving (1 tablespoon): *Calories 39 (From Fat 0); Fat 0g (Saturated 0g); Cholesterol 0mg; Sodium 2mg; Carbohydrate 10g (Dietary Fiber 1g); Protein 0g.*

Cherry-Dried Plum Jam

I've always liked dried plums. They are plump and sweet and taste great eaten straight out of the box or used in cooking. When combined with dried cherries, they make a delicious, thick jam that tastes of summer.

Preparation time: *10 minutes*

Cooking time: *5 minutes under pressure*

Pressure setting: *High*

Yield: *Approximately 5 cups*

1½ cups water	¼ pound dried pitted cherries
½ cup orange juice	1 pound (about 3 cups) pitted prunes, cut in half
½ cup sugar	

1 Bring the water and orange juice to a boil in a pressure cooker. Add the sugar and stir until dissolved. Add the dried cherries and prunes.

2 Cover and bring to high pressure over high heat. Lower the heat to stabilize the pressure. Cook for 5 minutes.

3 Remove from the heat. Release the pressure using a quick-release method.

4 Unlock and remove the cover. Using a handheld potato masher, gently mash the cooked fruit. Stir well. Refrigerate when cool.

Per serving (1 tablespoon): Calories 31 (From Fat 0); Fat 0g (Saturated 0g); Cholesterol 0mg; Sodium 1mg; Carbohydrate 8g (Dietary Fiber 1g); Protein 0g.

Cranberry-Orange Chutney

A nice departure from jellied cranberry sauce, my Cranberry-Orange Chutney is a pleasing balance of sweet and tart with just the right amount of spicy undertones. Serve this as an accompaniment to roast turkey or pork, or slather some on a sandwich made with leftover roast meat or poultry.

Preparation time: *10 minutes*

Cooking time: *5 minutes under pressure*

Pressure setting: *High*

Yield: *Approximately 8 cups*

½ cup orange juice

⅓ cup white wine vinegar

½ cup orange marmalade

1 cup sugar

½ cup packed light brown sugar

½ teaspoon ground ginger

¼ teaspoon cayenne pepper

½ teaspoon salt

1 cup toasted chopped walnuts (see the Tip at the end of the recipe)

1 bag (12 ounces) fresh or frozen cranberries

1 cup dried cranberries

1 small red onion, finely chopped

2 tablespoons grated orange zest

1 cinnamon stick

1 bay leaf

1 Combine the orange juice, vinegar, marmalade, sugar, brown sugar, ginger, cayenne pepper, and salt in a pressure cooker. Bring to a boil and stir until the sugar disolves. Add the walnuts, fresh cranberries, dried cranberries, onion, orange zest, cinnamon stick, and bay leaf. Stir together.

2 Cover and bring to high pressure over high heat. Lower the heat to stabilize the pressure. Cook for 5 minutes.

3 Remove from the heat. Release the pressure using a quick-release method.

4 Unlock and remove the cover. Stir well. Cool to room temperature and refrigerate.

Tip: *To toast walnuts, place them in a dry skillet over medium heat and cook, stirring or shaking the pan often so that they do not burn, about 3 to 4 minutes.*

Vary It! *For a thicker, more relishlike consistency, spoon the cutney mixture into the bowl of a food processor and a pulse a couple times until coarsely chopped.*

Per serving (1 tablespoon): *Calories 25 (From Fat 6); Fat 1g (Saturated 0g); Cholesterol 0mg; Sodium 10mg; Carbohydrate 5g (Dietary Fiber 0g); Protein 0g.*

Part V
The Part of Tens

"Hang on, everyone—I'll have your lunches out in a minute."

In this part...

Here I've assembled some of my favorite top ten lists, which include pressure cooking tips, stumbling blocks you may encounter (and their solutions), and Web sites that I'm certain you'll find as invaluable as I do.

Chapter 11

Ten Problems and How to Handle Them

In This Chapter

▶ Keeping your cool when things go wrong

▶ Knowing how to fix common problems

*B*ecause pressure cookers are relatively easy to use, with relatively few moving parts, they hardly ever break or malfunction. Nevertheless, things can go wrong, be it user or operational error, so I've compiled a list of ten problems that can occur, along with reasons and advice on how to keep the problems from happening again.

If you experience a problem that I don't touch upon, please consult the printed materials provided by the manufacturer of your pressure cooker. If you still can't find the solution to the problem, contact the company's customer service department. For a listing of manufacturers and their contact information, please see Appendix A.

Don't Force That Cover Closed!

Problem: You can't close the cover.

Reasons:

1. The cover isn't sitting squarely on top of the pressure cooker.

2. The rubber gasket isn't positioned properly under the cover.

Solutions:

1. The locking mechanism on most pressure cookers is similar to that of a jar. If positioned at an angle, it will not close. Make sure the cover is sitting squarely on top of the pressure cooker before trying to close it.

2. Before trying to close the pressure cooker, make sure that the gasket is positioned properly and is laying flat.

Once the cover is closed, you will hear a click once it locks in place.

Never force the cover closed, or you may not ever be able to open it again.

Anemic Pressure

Problem: The pressure indicator doesn't rise, or the jiggler valve doesn't turn with vim and vigor.

Reasons:

1. The burner isn't hot enough.
2. The recipe doesn't call for enough liquid to create steam.
3. The rubber gasket isn't positioned properly under the cover.
4. The pressure regulator valve is dirty or obstructed.
5. The pressure cooker was damaged, and the safety valve has activated or is blocked, inhibiting pressure from building up.

Solutions:

1. Raise the burner heat to high (make this a habit!) when bringing the pressure cooker up to pressure.
2. Always use at least 1 cup of cooking liquid, although some manufacturers suggest using at least 2 cups. Check the owner's manual to determine the correct amount needed for your model of pressure cooker.
3. Make sure that the rubber gasket is positioned properly under the cover.
4. Clean the pressure regulator valve according to the manufacturer's instructions in the owner's manual.
5. The safety valves kick in if the pressure cooker is damaged. Contact the manufacturer for after-sales service repair.

A Leaky Pot

Problem: Condensation or steam leaks from under the cover of the pressure cooker.

Reasons:

1. The cover isn't properly closed

2. The gasket isn't properly positioned or is damaged.

3. The pressure cooker is overfilled.

Solutions:

1. Release any pressure using a quick release method. Open and reclose the cover as discussed above in *Don't force that cover closed!*.

2. Release any pressure using a quick release method. Open the pressure cooker. Remove the gasket; check for tears or cracks. If damaged, replace the gasket. If it's okay, check the owner's manual to see if the gasket has to be positioned in a specific fashion or location, since some have small cutouts or openings which must be lined up in order for the pressure cooker to work properly.

3. Never fill the pressure cooker more than half full with liquid, or more than two-thirds full with food. If above the limit, remove excess and continue cooking under pressure.

Note: Small drops of condensation are normal on the lids of some pressure cookers.

The Key to Unlocking the Cover

Problem: You can't open or remove the cover.

Reasons:

1. There is still some pressure in the pressure cooker.

2. A vacuum has formed.

3. The cover wasn't positioned properly when closed.

Solutions:

1. Always release all of the pressure before attempting to open the lid.

2. If the lid will still not open after releasing all pressure, a vacuum may have formed. Bring the contents of the pot up to pressure again over high heat and then try releasing the pressure.

3. Never force the cover into locked position. If you still can't get the cover off, contact the manufacturer.

Just Broke My Tooth on a Pea

Problem: The food is undercooked.

Reasons:

1. The pressure cooker didn't reach or maintain pressure and thus didn't operate properly.

2. The food wasn't cooked long enough.

Solutions:

1. Always bring the pressure cooker up to pressure over high heat. The pressure indicator valve or the weighted valve must be in the upright position, or the jiggler valve must be turning with vim and vigor before you lower the burner to a simmer. After lowering the heat, make sure that the pressure cooker maintains pressure. If not, raise the burner heat a bit until it does.

2. Reposition the cover and cook for an additional 1 to 3 minutes (depending how hard or tough the food is) on high pressure. Release pressure and check the food.

That's the Mushiest Pot Roast I've Ever Eaten!

Problem: The food is overcooked.

Reason: The food was cooked too long under pressure

Solution: Make a note and reduce the cooking time when preparing the food next time.

For cooking time accuracy, always use a kitchen timer. Set the timer for the cooking time needed, once the pressure cooker reaches pressure.

Holy Smoke!

Problem: Food burns or sticks to the bottom of the pot.

Reasons:

1. There was'nt enough cooking liquid.

2. The burner heat was too high, causing food to stick to the bottom of the pot or the liquid to evaporate.

Solutions:

1. Check the recipe for the correct amount of cooking liquid.

2. Next time, be sure to reduce the burner heat to low once pressure is reached. On an electric cooktop, use two burners — one on high heat for reaching pressure and the other on low for maintaining it. Move the pressure cooker from the high burner to the low one after the cooker reaches high pressure.

 If you burn food on the bottom of the pressure cooker pot, remove as much of the food as possible and try cleaning with a non-abrasive cleaning such as Bon Ami.

1 Told You to Lower the Heat

Problem: The safety valves activate.

Reason: The pressure cooker reached the level of pressure chosen, and the burner heat wasn't lowered.

Solution: Never exceed the amount of pressure chosen; lower the burner heat once the desired level of pressure is reached.

Pressure without a Rise

Problem: The pressure indicator (on certain models only) doesn't rise as pressure builds.

Reason: The pressure indicator is dirty and therefore stuck.

Solution: Remove pressure cooker from stove. Release any pressure using a quick release method. Remove cover. Refer to the manufacturer's owner's manual for instructions on to clean the pressure indicator. Replace the cover. Place pressure cooker on stove and resume cooking.

Mirror, Mirror, on the Wall, Why Isn't My Pressure Cooker the Shiniest of All?

Problem: The metal finish is dull.

Reasons:

1. Certain high-acidity foods, such as tomatoes, interact with an aluminum pot and discolor the metal finish.

2. Hard water and foods such as dried beans can leave a cloudy cover on the bottom of the pressure cooker.

3. If the heat is too high in a dry pot, or in a pot with little food and liquid, that can cause scorching.

4. The outside of the pot was cleaned with abrasive cleaners or scouring pads.

Solutions:

1. This condition is normal. To minimize the effect, remove high-acidic foods from the pressure cooker immediately after cooking.

2. Soak the inside bottom of the pressure cooker pot with a solution made of two parts water and one part white vinegar. Let sit for 10 minutes before pouring out and rinsing.

3. Always make sure that there is liquid or oil in the pressure cooker pot as it heats up over medium-high, only. If there are scorch or burnt marks in the pressure cooker pot, try removing them with a non-abrasive cleaning powder like Bon Ami.

4. To keep the exterior finish of the pressure cooker shiny, I've learned over the years to never use common abrasive cleaners or scouring pads. Attempt to remove stains or burnt marks with a non-abrasive cleaning powder like Bon Ami.

Chapter 12

Ten Web Sites to Check Out

*H*ome computers are playing a significant role in how we cook and eat today. With cents-off coupons to download and print, opportunities to order ingredients and supplies, and recipes galore, numerous sites provide ongoing cooking assistance.

Pressure cookers are a popular Web site category. By searching for the words *pressure cookers* and *pressure cooker recipes,* I found hundreds of related sites. In this chapter, I've narrowed them down to ten of my favorites based on practicality, ease of access and use, and the quality of the recipes. I hope that you enjoy them as much as I do. Bear in mind, however, that Web sites change constantly; what is great today may very well be passé tomorrow, with something new and exciting just coming into play.

About.com

http://homecooking.about.com/food/homecooking/library/sub/ msubpressure.htm

An anthology of pressure cooker Web sites, About.com links you to nine other Web sites for an interesting collection of pressure cooker facts and trivia, as well as recipes from manufacturers and pressure cooker cookbooks. The quality of the material is quite good and well organized.

Diana's Kitchen

www.dianaskitchen.com/page/pressure.htm

A short but appealing list of contemporary recipes, including Maple Pecan Sweet Potatoes and Veal or Lamb Stew with Dumplings. Reading through this site reminds me of going through my recipe file box, where I save only the very best recipes.

Epinions.com

www.epinions.com/hmgd-Small_Appliances-All-Pressure_Cookers

In the market for a new pressure cooker, or perhaps you want to see what other consumers think of the brand and model you already own? Then this is the Web site for you. Epinions.com members have listed more than 40 different models of pressure cookers that they own and use. Each model is rated and, in most cases, has a lengthy owner/user review and critique. The information is well presented, and I found the comments and criticisms generally valid (I didn't see anyone with an ax to grind, which happens so frequently online). Just bear in mind that these are people's opinions and not those of a testing agency.

I like that the pressure cookers are listed in order of preference. Another nice feature is that you can check off a few different models listed on the same page, click on "Compare these items," and Epinions.com reformats the page so that you get a side-by-side comparison of the models you chose. Very cool!

Colorado State University Cooperative Extension Bureau

Colorado State University Cooperative Extension Bureau is a great resource for those who live and pressure-cook in high-altitude areas. For a concise yet detailed explanation, check out the following Web page:

www.ext.colostate.edu/pubs/columncc/cc970123.htm

In addition to pressure cookers used for cooking, larger versions, called pressure canners, are used to preserve or can foods under pressure, especially foods low in acidity. For more information, you may want to visit the following Web page:

www.ext.colostate.edu/pubs/columncc/cc970731.htm

ezboard

http://pub17.ezboard.com/fwhatscookinfrm6

This user-friendly recipe exchange Web site is a good place to gather ideas and new recipes. Even I was able to pick up some new information regarding pressure cooker Web sites. Be sure to read (and heed!) the comments on deep frying in a pressure cooker. A no-no!

The New Homemaker

www.newhomemaker.com/cooking/beans2.html

The New Homemaker provides homemakers with invaluable tips on everyday matters. Because beans are one of my all-time favorite foods to make in a pressure cooker, I was impressed with this page from the Web site: *Bean Recipes — From soup to fudge. Really.* Yes, there are recipes for making even chocolate fudge by using cooked pinto and black beans. Although the recipes are not pressure cooker–specific, you can easily use cooked beans from the Master Bean Recipe in Chapter 6 to make any of the recipes found at this page.

National Presto Industries, Inc., Pressure Cooking School Program

www.presto-net.com/school/toknow.html

One of the few remaining American manufacturers of pressure cookers, National Presto designed this Web site as a classroom tool for home economics and culinary arts teachers. Nevertheless, consumers who might have a question or two on pressure cooker use, cooking, and care can find some great material here. Presto pressure cookers use jiggler valves, so most of the operational information pertains to this type of pot. Because some of the pages deal with classroom activities, I've selected those that are for a more general interest. They include Pressure Pointers, Getting to Know the Pressure Cooker, and Getting to Know the Pressure Cooker Parts.

RecipeSource

www.recipesource.com

RecipeSource is home to SOAR (Searchable Online Archive of Recipes), an excellent cooking resource for all types of cooking with well over 70,000 recipes. Although there isn't a specific location for pressure cooker recipes, you can easily sort and access a list of pressure cooker recipes simply by typing the words **pressure cooker** in the *Search for Recipes* box and clicking GO. You're rewarded with close to 150 different entries covering the common to the exotic, including a recipe for kangaroo tail soup from Australia, which the submitter claims is "a family favourite."

spinnaweb.com Pressure Cooker Recipes

http://pressure.spinnaweb.com/index.html

This Web site seeks to be the only site you'll ever need for pressure cooker recipes and advice. The recipes, which run the gamut from entrees to desserts, need to be downloaded using Acrobat Reader. While the site's online Pressure Cooker Store naturally sells pressure cookers, it also carries pressure cooker–sized 7-inch springform baking pans, pudding molds, and so on.

vegetarian.about.com

http://vegetarian.about.com/food/vegetarian/library/weekly/aa091399.htm?terms=pressure+cookers

Cooking with pressure can be a lifesaver for busy vegetarian cooks who want to cook up an endless number of bean and grain dishes in addition to garden-fresh vegetables. With a concise list of vegetarian recipes, this site is great for delicious, quick, and easy-to-prepare appetizers, soups, stews, entrees, and desserts.

Chapter 13

Ten Tips for Great Pressure-Cooking

In This Chapter

▶ Getting the best results from your pressure cooker

▶ Overcoming common problems

*B*ecause pressure cookers cook differently than conventional covered pots do, you have to rethink some old cooking methods and master a couple of new tricks when using a pressure cooker, especially if you want delicious results every time. But don't be overwhelmed or perplexed. In this chapter, I share with you some things that you should be aware of before, during, and after cooking under pressure.

Keeping It Safe

Pressure-cooking today is a far cry from the methods used even 15 years ago. Pressure cookers are safer to use than ever before, especially if you follow my five-point inspection checklist (discussed in greater detail in Chapter 3) each and every time you use your:

1. **Keep the pressure cooker clean.** Always wash your pressure cooker well after use, or if you haven't used it for an extended period.

2. **Remove and inspect the rubber sealing gasket or ring before using the pressure cooker.**

3. **Check the safety valves to make sure that they're clean and in good working order.** Consult your owner's manual for the exact procedures.

4. **Fill the pressure cooker properly; do not overfill it, and be sure to use enough liquid.**

5. **Look, listen, and smell as the pressure cooker cooks.** If you see excess steam or condensation coming out of the valves or from under the cover; if you hear steam escaping from the safety valves; or if you smell the food burning, remove the pressure cooker from the stove and immediately release the pressure by using a quick release method as described in Chapter 2.

Determining What a Pressure Cooker Can Hold

Even though I developed and tested the recipes in this book in 6-quart pressure cookers, you never fill a 6-quart pot with more than 4 quarts of food. Even though steam weighs nothing, it requires space as it builds up. Therefore, regardless of the pressure cooker's size:

- Never fill it more than ⅔ full with food.
- Never fill it more than halfway with liquid.

See Chapter 2 for a more in-depth discussion of filling a pressure cooker.

Using Enough Liquid

A pressure cooker cooks under pressure by bringing cooking liquid to a boil in a sealed pot that traps the building steam, causing the temperature inside the closed pressure cooker to rise to 250 degrees. To get this process to work, you must cook with at least 1 cup of cooking liquid, although check the manufacturer's owners manual since some pressure cookers may need up to 2 cups of liquid. Nevertheless, never fill a pressure cooker more than half full with cooking liquid.

Intensifying Flavors by Searing and Browning First

Today, many people have less-than-fond memories of the food their mothers or grandmothers made in pressure cookers. For whatever reason, a couple of generations ago, overcooked, mushy food was pretty much the norm. Pressure cookers helped the home cook make that happen even quicker! Food was thrown in the pressure cooker pot with an abundance of liquid and cooked about twice as long as needed. The end result: gray, unrecognizable foods! Nowadays, we like to eat our veggies brightly colored and somewhat crunchy and our meat flavorful and still intact.

To get the maximum flavor out of foods cooked in a pressure cooker, I like to sear and brown them first in a small amount of oil to intensify the flavor and overall appeal. Always do so in the pressure cooker pot before cooking under pressure. Foods that benefit greatly from this technique include meat and poultry for stews and braised dishes, as well as vegetables like squash, eggplant, onions, tomatoes, and bell peppers.

Pressure-Cooking at High Altitudes

Because foods generally cook slower at higher altitudes, quick-cooking under pressure is a dream come true for most mountain dwellers.Water and cooking liquids come to a boil slower at higher altitudes; therefore, high-pressure-cooking times need to be longer. A good general rule is to increase the cooking time by 5 percent for every 1,000 feet you are above the first 2,000 feet above sea level. Table 13-1 provides information for you to use as a guide.

Table 13-1	High-Altitude Cooking Time Adjustments
Altitude in Feet	*Increase in Cooking Times*
3,000	5%
4,000	10%
5,000	15%
6,000	20%
7,000	25%
8,000	30%

The recipes in this book were developed and tested at sea level. If you live at an altitude of 3,000 feet or higher, remember to adjust the given recipe cook times according to Table 13-1.

Building the Right Amount of Pressure

After the pressure cooker lid is positioned and locked, you're ready to get down to the business of cooking under pressure. In order to build pressure, you must have a combination of heat and liquid. You can't have one without the other.

If your pressure cooker is a jiggler valve or weighted valve type, the weight has to be on the vent pipe. If you have a spring regulator valve pressure cooker with a pressure level indicator, it has to be set on the level of pressure you want.

Set the pressure cooker over high heat. When you begin to exceed pressure, lower the burner heat to a simmer — or play "burner hopscotch" (see Chapter 3). Now set the timer for the length of time you need to cook and *voila!* you're pressure-cooking!

Releasing Pressure without Burning Yourself

Choose the appropriate steam release method for the type of food you're cooking. Use a Quick Release Method if steam needs to be released immediately. Use the Natural Release Method only when preparing foods such as pot roast or stock that will benefit from the extended time in the pressure cooker as the pressure drops on its own.

Steam is hot, especially when coming out of a pressure cooker. It usually comes out of the pressure indicator or regulator valve. Check your pressure cooker owner's manual to see where these are located and make sure you always release the steam away from you, never toward you.

If your pressure cooker has a steam release setting or switch, liquid may sometimes spray out the pressure regulator valve along with the steam. To avoid having to clean tomato sauce or bean cooking liquid off your wall or stove, switch the pressure regulator valve back to high pressure. Release pressure in the sink using the Cold Water Release Method.

Avoiding the "Too Hard" Scenario

Remember that hard food is better than mushy food; you can always cook it longer with or without pressure! You can do a few things, however, to get whatever you're cooking done right the first time.

- Cut food into uniformly sized shapes.

- Because steam needs to circulate around the food, never pack food into the pressure cooker.

- Never overfill the pressure cooker pot.

- Batch-cook the food: First cook foods that need more time to cook; then release pressure and add the faster-cooking foods. (See Chapter 3 for more information on "stop-and-go cooking.")

- Never add salt to soaked, dried beans when cooking. The skin will never soften and may even toughen.

- Cook for the recommended length of time.

See Chapter 11 for more information about avoiding underdone foods.

Avoiding the "Too Soft" Scenario

Nothing is worse than mushy, tasteless, overcooked food. You can avoid overcooking your favorites in your pressure cooker by following a few simple rules:

- Never cook food in more cooking liquid than the recipe specifies.

- Never cook naturally soft or tender foods in a pressure cooker. Why bother? They'll only come out softer and mushier! Some things I've learned to avoid (the hard way!) are fish fillets, most shellfish (except live lobster), and snap peas.

- Cook for the recommended length of time.

- Don't hesitate to release the pressure after cooking. Even if you remove the pressure cooker from the stove, the food continues cooking as long as there is heat and pressure in the pot.

See Chapter 11 for more information about avoiding overdone foods.

Keeping It Clean

Pot looking dull? Valves a bit sluggish? Gasket frayed around the edges? You'll never get up to pressure if you don't take proper care of your pressure cooker.

Always hand-wash the pressure cooker after each use with mild dishwashing soap and a nonabrasive sponge or cloth. Remove all caked-on food particles. Towel-dry well before storing. Replace the rubber gasket the minute it begins to look worn or damaged. See Chapter 3 for more details on cleaning your pressure cooker.

Contact Information for Pressure Cooker Manufacturers

• •

*O*ccasionally, you may need to contact the manufacturer of your pressure cooker. The following list of the most popular brands of pressure cookers provides you with the manufacturer's customer service address, phone number, and Web site or e-mail address. Because warranty and return policies vary from manufacturer to manufacturer, I suggest that you always check with the customer service department before sending anything back for repair or exchange.

Fagor (Cook's Essentials Pressure Cookers)

Fagor America, Inc.
P.O. Box 94
Lyndhurst, NJ 07071
Phone: 800-207-0806
Web site: www.fagoramerica.com
E-mail: info@fagoramerica.com

Hawkins Futura

Bay City International
P.O. Box 11706
Green Bay, WI 54307
Phone: 920-339-0510
Web site: www.pressurecooker.com
E-mail: baycity gb@aol.com

Innova

Customer Service
Innova, Inc.
409 West 76th Street
Davenport, IA 52806
Phone: 800-767-5160
Web site/e-mail access: www.innova-inc.com

Kuhn Rikon (Duromatic Pressure Cookers)

Kuhn Rikon Corporation
350 Bon Air Center #240
Greenbrae, CA 94904
Phone: 415-461-3927
Web site: www.kuhnrikon.com
E-mail: kuhnrikon@kuhnrikon.com

Manttra

Manttra, Inc.
5721 Bayside Road, Suite J
Virginia Beach, VA 23455
Phone: 877-962-6887
Fax: 757-318-7604
Web site/E-mail access: www.manttra.com

Magafesa

North American Promotions, Ltd.
1232 West NW Highway
Palatine, IL 60067
Phone: 888-787-9991
Web site: www.noampro.com
E-mail: napl@interaccess.com

Mirro

Consumer Center
Mirro Company
1512 Washington St.
Manitowoc, WI 54220
Phone: 800-527-7727
Web site: www.mirro.com
E-mail: moreinfo@mirro.com

Presto

Consumer Service Department
National Presto Industries, Inc.
3925 North Hastings Way
Eau Claire, WI 54703-2209
Phone: 800-877-0441
Web site: www.presto.net.com
E-mail: contact@GoPresto.com

T-Fal

Consumer Relations
T-Fal Corporation
25 Riverside Drive
Pine Brook, NJ 07058
Phone: 800-395-8325
Web site: www.t-falusa.com
E-mail: askt-fal@t-fal.com

Appendix B

Metric Conversion Guide

● ●

*N**ote:* The recipes in this cookbook were not developed or tested using metric measures. There may be some variation in quality when converting to metric units.

Common Abbreviations

Abbreviation(s)	What It Stands For
C, c	cup
g	gram
kg	kilogram
L, l	liter
lb	pound
mL, ml	milliliter
oz	ounce
pt	pint
t, tsp	teaspoon
T, TB, Tbl, Tbsp	tablespoon

Volume

U.S. Units	Canadian Metric	Australian Metric
¼ teaspoon	1 mL	1 ml
½ teaspoon	2 mL	2 ml
1 teaspoon	5 mL	5 ml
1 tablespoon	15 mL	20 ml

(continued)

Volume *(continued)*

U.S. Units	Canadian Metric	Australian Metric
¼ cup	50 mL	60 ml
⅓ cup	75 mL	80 ml
½ cup	125 mL	125 ml
⅔ cup	150 mL	170 ml
¾ cup	175 mL	190 ml
1 cup	250 mL	250 ml
1 quart	1 liter	1 liter
1½ quarts	1.5 liters	1.5 liters
2 quarts	2 liters	2 liters
2½ quarts	2.5 liters	2.5 liters
3 quarts	3 liters	3 liters
4 quarts	4 liters	4 liters

Weight

U.S. Units	Canadian Metric	Australian Metric
1 ounce	30 grams	30 grams
2 ounces	55 grams	60 grams
3 ounces	85 grams	90 grams
4 ounces (¼ pound)	115 grams	125 grams
8 ounces (½ pound)	225 grams	225 grams
16 ounces (1 pound)	455 grams	500 grams
1 pound	455 grams	1/2 kilogram

Measurements

Inches	Centimeters
½	1.5
1	2.5

Inches	Centimeters
2	5.0
3	7.5
4	10.0
5	12.5
6	15.0
7	17.5
8	20.5
9	23.0
10	25.5
11	28.0
12	30.5
13	33.0

Temperature (Degrees)

Fahrenheit	Celsius
32	0
212	100
250	120
275	140
300	150
325	160
350	180
375	190
400	200
425	220
450	230
475	240
500	260

Appendix C

Common Substitutions, Abbreviations, and Equivalents

● ●

*T*hings don't always go as planned in the kitchen. Even pros get caught shorthanded once in a while. We can't tell you how many times we thought that we had a specific ingredient only to find out halfway through making a recipe that this ingredient had mysteriously vanished.

This chapter can help get you out of these jams. Sometimes, you can't use a substitute for an ingredient. For example, you can't make a cake recipe that calls for flour without the flour. However, many times you can make some adjustments. For example, vegetable oil can almost always replace olive oil. The flavor may not be as good, but the recipe works. Likewise, you can surely make a recipe that calls for walnuts using pecans or almonds instead.

Here are some not-so-obvious substitutions that you can make when in a pinch. Remember, it's always best to follow a recipe. But when you can't, turn to this list for help.

For thickening soups, stews, and sauces:

- 1 tablespoon (15 milliliters) cornstarch or potato starch = 2 tablespoons (30 milliliters) all-purpose flour
- 1 tablespoon (15 milliliters) arrowroot = 2½ tablespoons (37 milliliters) all-purpose flour

For leavening agents in baked goods:

- ¼ teaspoon (1 milliliter) baking soda + ½ teaspoon (2 milliliters) cream of tartar = 1 teaspoon (5 milliliters) double-acting baking powder
- ¼ teaspoon (1 milliliter) baking soda + ½ cup (125 milliliters) buttermilk or plain yogurt = 1 teaspoon (5 milliliters) double-acting baking powder in liquid mixtures only; reduce liquid in recipe by ½ cup (125 milliliters)

For dairy products:

- 1 cup (250 milliliters) whole milk = ½ cup (125 milliliters) evaporated milk + ½ cup (125 milliliters) water

  or 1 cup (250 milliliters) skim milk + 2 tablespoons (30 milliliters) melted butter

  or ¼ cup (50 milliliters) powdered milk + 1 cup (250 milliliters) water

  or 1 cup (250 milliliters) soy milk

For eggs:

- 2 egg yolks = 1 whole egg
- 4 extra-large eggs = 5 large eggs

For sweetening:

- 1 cup brown sugar = 1 cup (250 milliliters) granulated sugar + 1½ tablespoons (22 milliliters) molasses

Miscellaneous substitutions:

- 1 tablespoon (15 milliliters) prepared mustard = 1 teaspoon (5 milliliters) dried mustard
- 1 cup (250 milliliters) broth or stock = 1 bouillon cube dissolved in 1 cup (250 milliliters) boiling water
- 1 square (1 ounce/28 grams) unsweetened chocolate = 3 tablespoons (45 milliliters) unsweetened cocoa + 1 tablespoon (15 milliliters) butter, margarine, vegetable shortening, or oil
- 1 ounce (28 grams) semisweet chocolate = 3 tablespoons (45 milliliters) unsweetened cocoa + 2 tablespoons (30 milliliters) butter, margarine, vegetable shortening, or oil + 3 tablespoons (45 milliliters) granulated sugar

Suppose that a recipe calls for 1 pound tomatoes, and you don't own a kitchen scale. (You should, you know.) Or maybe you can't remember how many tablespoons are in a cup. Table C-1 lists common equivalent measures. Table C-2 deals with food items, giving cup and weight measures for some often-used ingredients. All measurements are for level amounts. Note that some metric measurements are approximate.

Table C-1	Conversion Secrets	
This Measurement . . .	*. . . Equals This Measurement . . .*	*. . . Equals This Measurement*
Pinch or dash	less than ⅛ teaspoon	0.5 mL
3 teaspoons	1 tablespoon	15 mL
2 tablespoons	1 fluid ounce	30 mL
4 tablespoons	¼ cup	50 mL
5 tablespoons	⅓ cup	75 mL + 1 teaspoon
8 tablespoons	½ cup	100 mL
10 tablespoons	⅔ cup	150 mL + 2 teaspoons
12 tablespoons	¾ cup	175 mL
16 tablespoons	1 cup	250 mL
1 cup	8 fluid ounces	250 mL
2 cups	1 pint or 16 fluid ounces	500 mL
2 pints	1 quart or 32 fluid ounces	1 L
4 quarts	1 gallon	4 L

Table C-2	Food Equivalents	
This Measurement . . .	*. . . Equals This Measurement . . .*	*. . . Equals This Measurement*
1 pound all-purpose flour	4 cups sifted	1 L sifted
3 medium apples or bananas	approximately 1 pound	500 g
2 slices bread	1 cup fresh bread crumbs	250 mL
1 pound brown sugar	2¼ cups packed	550 mL packed
8 tablespoons butter	1 stick	125 mL or ½ cup
4 sticks butter	1 pound	454 g

(continued)

Table C-2 *(continued)*

This Measurement...	... Equals This Measurement...	... Equals This Measurement
6 ounces chocolate chips	1 cup	250 mL
1 pound confectioners sugar	4½ cups sifted	1.125 L sifted
1 cup dried beans	2 cups cooked	500 mL
1 large garlic clove minced	approximately 1 teaspoon	5 mL minced
1 pound granulated sugar	2 cups	500 mL
½ pound hard cheese (such as Parmesan)	approximately 2 cups grated	500 mL grated
1 cup heavy whipping cream	2 cups whipped	500 mL whipped
1 medium lemon	3 tablespoons juice, 1 to 2 teaspoons grated peel	45 mL juice, 5 to 10 mL grated peel
4 ounces nuts	approximately ⅔ cup chopped	150 mL chopped
1 large onion	approximately 1 cup chopped	250 mL chopped
1 pound pasta	4 cups raw, 8 cups cooked	1 L raw, 2 L cooked
3 medium potatoes	approximately 1 pound	500 g
1 cup raw rice	3 cups cooked	750 mL cooked
1 large tomato	approximately ¾ cup chopped	175 mL chopped
3 medium tomatoes	approximately 1 pound	500 g
1 28-ounce can whole tomatoes	3½ cups	875 mL

Index

• T •

• U •

• V •

Notes

Notes

Notes

FOR DUMMIES®

The easy way to get more done and have more fun

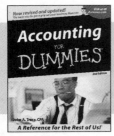

FOR DUMMIES®

A world of resources to help you grow

HOME, GARDEN & HOBBIES

Feng Shui FOR DUMMIES
0-7645-5295-3

Gardening FOR DUMMIES
0-7645-5130-2

Guitar FOR DUMMIES
0-7645-5106-X

Also available:

Auto Repair For Dummies
(0-7645-5089-6)

Chess For Dummies
(0-7645-5003-9)

Home Maintenance For Dummies
(0-7645-5215-5)

Organizing For Dummies
(0-7645-5300-3)

Piano For Dummies
(0-7645-5105-1)

Poker For Dummies
(0-7645-5232-5)

Quilting For Dummies
(0-7645-5118-3)

Rock Guitar For Dummies
(0-7645-5356-9)

Roses For Dummies
(0-7645-5202-3)

Sewing For Dummies
(0-7645-5137-X)

FOOD & WINE

Cooking FOR DUMMIES
0-7645-5250-3

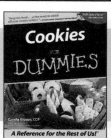

Cookies FOR DUMMIES
0-7645-5390-9

Wine FOR DUMMIES
0-7645-5114-0

Also available:

Bartending For Dummies
(0-7645-5051-9)

Chinese Cooking For Dummies
(0-7645-5247-3)

Christmas Cooking For Dummies
(0-7645-5407-7)

Diabetes Cookbook For Dummies
(0-7645-5230-9)

Grilling For Dummies
(0-7645-5076-4)

Low-Fat Cooking For Dummies
(0-7645-5035-7)

Slow Cookers For Dummies
(0-7645-5240-6)

TRAVEL

Italy FOR DUMMIES
0-7645-5453-0

Hawaii FOR DUMMIES
0-7645-5438-7

Las Vegas FOR DUMMIES
0-7645-5448-4

Also available:

America's National Parks For Dummies
(0-7645-6204-5)

Caribbean For Dummies
(0-7645-5445-X)

Cruise Vacations For Dummies 2003
(0-7645-5459-X)

Europe For Dummies
(0-7645-5456-5)

Ireland For Dummies
(0-7645-6199-5)

France For Dummies
(0-7645-6292-4)

London For Dummies
(0-7645-5416-6)

Mexico's Beach Resorts For Dummies
(0-7645-6262-2)

Paris For Dummies
(0-7645-5494-8)

RV Vacations For Dummies
(0-7645-5443-3)

Walt Disney World & Orlando For Dummies
(0-7645-5444-1)

Available wherever books are sold. Go to www.dummies.com or call 1-877-762-2974 to order direct.

FOR DUMMIES®

Helping you expand your horizons and realize your potential

INTERNET

0-7645-0894-6

0-7645-1659-0

0-7645-1642-6

Also available:

America Online 7.0 For Dummies
(0-7645-1624-8)

Genealogy Online For Dummies
(0-7645-0807-5)

The Internet All-in-One Desk Reference For Dummies
(0-7645-1659-0)

Internet Explorer 6 For Dummies
(0-7645-1344-3)

The Internet For Dummies Quick Reference
(0-7645-1645-0)

Internet Privacy For Dummies
(0-7645-0846-6)

Researching Online For Dummies
(0-7645-0546-7)

Starting an Online Business For Dummies
(0-7645-1655-8)

DIGITAL MEDIA

0-7645-1664-7

0-7645-1675-2

0-7645-0806-7

Also available:

CD and DVD Recording For Dummies
(0-7645-1627-2)

Digital Photography All-in-One Desk Reference For Dummies
(0-7645-1800-3)

Digital Photography For Dummies Quick Reference
(0-7645-0750-8)

Home Recording for Musicians For Dummies
(0-7645-1634-5)

MP3 For Dummies
(0-7645-0858-X)

Paint Shop Pro "X" For Dummies
(0-7645-2440-2)

Photo Retouching & Restoration For Dummies
(0-7645-1662-0)

Scanners For Dummies
(0-7645-0783-4)

GRAPHICS

0-7645-0817-2

0-7645-1651-5

0-7645-0895-4

Also available:

Adobe Acrobat 5 PDF For Dummies
(0-7645-1652-3)

Fireworks 4 For Dummies
(0-7645-0804-0)

Illustrator 10 For Dummies
(0-7645-3636-2)

QuarkXPress 5 For Dummies
(0-7645-0643-9)

Visio 2000 For Dummies
(0-7645-0635-8)

Available wherever books are sold. Go to www.dummies.com or call 1-877-762-2974 to order direct.

FOR DUMMIES®

The advice and explanations you need to succeed

SELF-HELP, SPIRITUALITY & RELIGION

0-7645-5302-X

0-7645-5418-2

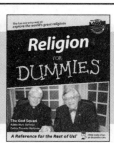

0-7645-5264-3

Also available:

The Bible For Dummies
(0-7645-5296-1)

Buddhism For Dummies
(0-7645-5359-3)

Christian Prayer For Dummies
(0-7645-5500-6)

Dating For Dummies
(0-7645-5072-1)

Judaism For Dummies
(0-7645-5299-6)

Potty Training For Dummies
(0-7645-5417-4)

Pregnancy For Dummies
(0-7645-5074-8)

Rekindling Romance For Dummies
(0-7645-5303-8)

Spirituality For Dummies
(0-7645-5298-8)

Weddings For Dummies
(0-7645-5055-1)

PETS

0-7645-5255-4

0-7645-5286-4

0-7645-5275-9

Also available:

Labrador Retrievers For Dummies
(0-7645-5281-3)

Aquariums For Dummies
(0-7645-5156-6)

Birds For Dummies
(0-7645-5139-6)

Dogs For Dummies
(0-7645-5274-0)

Ferrets For Dummies
(0-7645-5259-7)

German Shepherds For Dummies
(0-7645-5280-5)

Golden Retrievers For Dummies
(0-7645-5267-8)

Horses For Dummies
(0-7645-5138-8)

Jack Russell Terriers For Dummies
(0-7645-5268-6)

Puppies Raising & Training Diary For Dummies
(0-7645-0876-8)

EDUCATION & TEST PREPARATION

0-7645-5194-9

0-7645-5325-9

0-7645-5210-4

Also available:

Chemistry For Dummies
(0-7645-5430-1)

English Grammar For Dummies
(0-7645-5322-4)

French For Dummies
(0-7645-5193-0)

The GMAT For Dummies
(0-7645-5251-1)

Inglés Para Dummies
(0-7645-5427-1)

Italian For Dummies
(0-7645-5196-5)

Research Papers For Dummies
(0-7645-5426-3)

The SAT I For Dummies
(0-7645-5472-7)

U.S. History For Dummies
(0-7645-5249-X)

World History For Dummies
(0-7645-5242-2)

FOR DUMMIES®

We take the mystery out of complicated subjects